BUILDING ELASTIC AND RESILIENT CLOUD APPLICATIONS

Building Elastic and Resilient Cloud Applications

Developer's Guide to the Enterprise Library
Integration Pack for Windows Azure™

Authors

Dominic Betts

Jérémi Bourgault

Julian Dominguez

Ercenk Keresteci

Grigori Melnik

Fernando Simonazzi

Erwin van der Valk

ISBN: 978-1-62114-000-9

Contents

FOREWORD   ix

PREFACE   xiii
  Who This Book Is For   xiv
  Why This Book Is Pertinent Now   xiv
  How This Book Is Structured   xv
  What You Need to Use the Code   xv
  Who's Who   xvi

ACKNOWLEDGMENTS   xix
  The Team Who Brought You This Guide   xix
  The Enterprise Library Integration Pack
    for Windows Azure Development Team xix
  Advisors   xx
    Advisory Council   xx
    Community   xx

1 Introduction to Windows Azure   1
  About Windows Azure   1
    Windows Azure Services and Features 3
      Compute Environment   3
      Data Management   4
      Networking Services   5
      Other Services   7
  Developing Windows Azure Applications   7
  Managing, Monitoring, and Debugging
    Windows Azure Applications   8
    Managing SQL Azure Databases   9
    Upgrading Windows Azure Applications 9
  Windows Azure Subscription and Billing Model 10
    Estimating Your Costs   12
  More Information   12

2 Introduction to Enterprise Library Integration Pack for Windows Azure 17
What Is Enterprise Library? 17
What Is the Enterprise Library Integration Pack for Windows Azure? 20
More Information 21

3 The Tailspin Scenario 23
The Tailspin Company 23
    Tailspin's Strategy 24
    The Surveys Application 24
    Tailspin's Goals and Concerns 26
The Surveys Application Architecture 27
More Information 29

4 Autoscaling and Windows Azure 31
What is Autoscaling? 31
What is the Autoscaling Application Block? 32
    Instance Autoscaling 34
    Application Throttling 35
    Rules and Actions 36
        Constraint Rules 36
        Reactive Rules 39
    Logging 42
    The Autoscaling Lifecycle 43
        Determine Requirements and Constraints 44
        Specify Rules 44
        Run the Application 44
        Collect and Analyze the Results 44
When Should You Use the Autoscaling Application Block? 45
    You Want Your Application to Respond Automatically to Changes in Demand 45
    You Want to Manage the Costs Associated with Running Your Application 45
    You Have Predictable Times When Your Application Requires Additional Resources 46
    When Should You Not Use the Autoscaling Application Block 46
        Simple Applications 46
        Controlling Costs 47
        Applications That Are Not Scalable 47
Using the Autoscaling Application Block 47
    Adding the Autoscaling Application Block to Your Visual Studio Project 49

Hosting the Autoscaling Application Block 50
Changes to Your Windows Azure
Application 51
The Service Information 52
Adding Throttling Behavior
to Your Application 54
Using Instance Autoscaling and Throttling Together 54
The Autoscaling Rules 55
Implementing Schedule-based Autoscaling
Without Reactive Rules 57
Monitoring the Autoscaling
Application Block 58
Advanced Usage Scenarios 60
Scale Groups 60
Using Notifications 62
Integrating with the Application Lifecycle 63
Extending the Autoscaling Application Block 65
Using the WASABiCmdlets 66
Sample Configuration Settings 67
Average Rule Evaluation Period 69
Long Rule Evaluation Period 70
Configuring the Stabilizer 70
Using the Planning Tool 72
How the Autoscaling Application Block Works 73
The Metronome 74
The Data Collectors 74
The Service Information Store 75
The Data Points Store 75
The Rule Evaluator 75
The Rules Store 75
The Logger 76
The Scaler 76
The Tracker 76
More Information 77

5   **Making Tailspin Surveys More Elastic** 83
The Premise 83
Goals and Requirements 84
Overview of the Autoscaling Solution 86
Using the Autoscaling Application Block
in Tailspin Surveys 86
Features of the Autoscaling Application Block 86
Hosting the Autoscaling Application Block
in Tailspin Surveys 87
Scale Groups in Tailspin Surveys 88

Autoscaling Rules in Tailspin Surveys 88
Collecting Autoscaling History Data
in Tailspin Surveys 91
An Autoscaling Configuration UI 92
Notifying Operators by SMS When
a Scaling Operation Takes Place 92
Inside the Implementation 92
Enabling the Autoscaling Application Block
to Read from the .cscfg File 93
Tailspin's Service Information Definition 93
Tailspin's Autoscaling Rules 95
Tailspin Surveys Constraint Rules 95
Tailspin Surveys Reactive Scaling Rules 96
Tailspin Surveys Reactive Throttling Rules 99
Tailspin Surveys Operands 101
Collecting Performance Counter Data
from Tailspin Surveys 102
Implementing Throttling Behavior 105
Editing and Saving Rules 107
Discovering the Location of the Rules Store 107
Reading and Writing to the Rules Store 107
Creating Valid Autoscaling Rules 109
Validating Target Names in the Rule Definitions 110
Editing and Saving the Service
Information 111
Visualizing the Autoscaling Actions 111
Implementing a Custom Action 115
Integrating a Custom Action with the
Autoscaling Application Block 115
Integrating a Custom Action with the
Tailspin Surveys Rule Editor 118
Implementing Custom Operands 119
Integrating a Custom Operand with the
Autoscaling Application Block 119
Integrating a Custom Operand with the
Tailspin Surveys Rule Editor 124
Configuring Logging in Tailspin Surveys 124
Setup and Physical Deployment 126
Certificates and Tailspin Surveys

Deployment   126
    Deploying a Service Certificate to Enable SSL   126
    Deploying the Management Certificate
      to Enable Scaling Operations   127
  Deploying Tailspin Surveys in Multiple
    Geographic Locations   128
    Data Transfer Costs   130
    Role Instances   131
    Configuration Differences   131
    Application Differences   131
More Information   132

6 Transient Fault Handling   133
What Are Transient Faults?   133
What Is the Transient Fault Handling
  Application Block?   134
    Historical Note   135
Using the Transient Fault Handling
Application Block   136
    Adding the Transient Fault Handling Application
      Block to Your Visual Studio Project   136
    Instantiating the Transient Fault
      Handling Application Block Objects   137
    Defining a Retry Strategy   137
    Defining a Retry Policy   138
    Executing an Operation
      with a Retry Policy   139
When Should You Use the Transient
Fault Handling Application Block?   140
    You are Using a Windows Azure Service   140
    You Are Using a Custom Service   140
More Information   141

7 Making Tailspin Surveys More Resilient   143
The Premise   143
Goals and Requirements   144
Overview of the Transient Fault Handling
  Application Block Solution   144
Inside the Implementation   145
Setup and Physical Deployment   148
More Information   148

APPENDICES

A   Sample Configurations For Deploying
  Tailspin Surveys To Multiple Data Centers   149
  Option 1   149
    Service Model   149
    Rules   151
  Option 2   154
    Service Model   155
    Rules   156

B   Tailspin Surveys Installation Guide   159
  Introduction   159
    Prerequisites   160
    Install Source Code and Dependencies   160
  Prepare Your Windows Azure Subscription
    for Deployment   162
    Generate the Windows Azure Management
      Certificate and Export as .pfx File   162
    Generate the SSL Certificate   165
    Create the Required Hosted Services   167
    Upload Certificates as Hosted Services'
      Service Certificates   169
    Create the Storage Account   170
  Building the Solution   172
    Install NuGet Packages   172
    Modify the Certificates in the Visual Studio
      Cloud Projects   173
    Prepare the Settings in the Cloud Projects   175
    Build the Solution   177
  Deploy to Windows Azure   178
    Deploying Tailspin to the Staging Slot   178
    Testing If Tailspin Surveys Works   180
      Public Website   180
      Tenant Website   180
      Management Website   180
  Configuring Tailspin Autoscaling Functionality   181
    Configuring the Service Information Store   181
    Uploading the Sample Rules   182
  Running Tailspin Surveys Locally in Debug Mode   182
  Running the Management Application
    in Simulated Mode   183
  Known Issues   184
  More Information   185

C   GLOSSARY   187

Foreword

Energy use in the IT sector is growing faster than in any other industry as society becomes ever more dependent on the computational and storage capabilities provided by data centers. Unfortunately, a combination of inefficient equipment, outdated operating practices, and lack of incentives means that much of the energy used in traditional data centers is wasted.

Most IT energy efficiency efforts have focused on physical infrastructure—deploying more energy-efficient computer hardware and cooling systems, using operating system power management features, and reducing the number of servers in data centers through hardware virtualization.

But a significant amount of this wasted energy stems from how applications are designed and operated. Most applications are provisioned with far more IT resources than they need, as a buffer to ensure acceptable performance and to protect against hardware failure. Most often, the actual needs of the application are simply never measured, analyzed, or reviewed.

Once the application is deployed with more resources than it typically needs, there is very little incentive for the application developers to instrument their application to make capacity planning easier. And when users start complaining that the application is performing slowly, it's often easier (and cheaper) to simply assign more resources to the application. Very rarely are these resources ever removed, even after demand for the application subsides.

Cloud computing has the potential to break this dynamic of over-provisioning applications. Because cloud platforms like Windows Azure charge for resource use in small increments (compute-hours) on a pay-as-you-go basis, developers can now have a direct and controllable impact on IT costs and associated resource use.

Applications that are designed to dynamically grow and shrink their resource use in response to actual and anticipated demand are not only less expensive to operate, but are significantly more efficient with their use of IT resources than traditional applications. Developers can also reduce hosting costs by scheduling background tasks to run during less busy periods when the minimum amount of resources are assigned to the application.

While the cloud provides great opportunities for saving money on hosting costs, developing a cloud application that relies on other cloud services is not without its challenges. One particular problem that developers have to deal with is "transient faults." Although infrequent, applications have to be tolerant of intermittent connectivity and responsiveness problems in order to be considered reliable and provide a good user experience.

Until now, developers on Windows Azure had to develop these capabilities on their own. With the release of the *Enterprise Library Integration Pack for Windows Azure*, developers can now easily build robust and resource efficient applications that can be intelligently scaled, and throttled. In addition, these applications can handle transient faults.

The first major component contained within the Integration Pack is the *Autoscaling Application Block*, otherwise known as "WASABi." This application block helps developers improve responsiveness and control Windows Azure costs by automatically scaling the number of web and worker roles in Windows Azure through dynamic provisioning and decommissioning of role instances across multiple hosted services. WASABi also provides mechanisms to help control resource use without scaling role instances through application throttling. Developers can use this application block to intelligently schedule or defer background processing to keep the number of role instances within certain boundaries and take advantage of idle periods.

One of the major advantages of WASABi is its extensibility, which makes your solutions much more flexible. Staying true to the design principles of other application blocks, WASABi provides a mechanism for plugging in your own custom metrics and calling custom actions. With these, you can design a rule set that takes into account your business scenarios and not just standard performance counters available through the Windows Azure Diagnostics.

The optimizing stabilizer will ensure that you do not end up scaling too quickly. It can also make sure scale actions correspond to the most optimal compute hour pricing charges. For applications that expect significant usage beyond more than a few instances, this application block will help developers save money on hosting costs while improving the "green credentials" of their application. It will also help your application meet target SLAs.

The other major component is the *Transient Fault Handling Application Block* (also known as "Topaz") that helps developers make their applications more robust by providing the logic for detecting and handling transient fault conditions for a number of common cloud-based services.

More than ever before, developers have an important role to play in controlling IT costs and improving IT energy efficiency, without sacrificing reliability. The Enterprise Library Integration Pack for Windows Azure can assist them in rapidly building Windows Azure-based applications that are reliable, resource efficient, and cost effective.

The Developer's Guide you are holding in your hands is written by the engineering team who designed and produced this integration pack. It is full of useful guidance and tips to help you learn quickly. Importantly, the coverage includes not only conceptual topics, but the concrete steps taken to make the accompanying reference implementation (Tailspin Surveys) more elastic, robust, and resilient.

Moreover, the guidance from the Microsoft patterns & practices team is not only encapsulated in the Developer's Guide and the reference implementation. Since the pack ships its source code and all its unit tests, a lot can be learned by examining those artifacts.

I highly recommend both the Enterprise Library Integration Pack for Windows Azure and this Developer's Guide to architects, software developers, administrators, and product owners who design new or migrate existing applications to Windows Azure. The practical advice contained in this book will help make your applications highly scalable and robust.

Mark Aggar, Senior Director
Environmental Sustainability
Microsoft Corporation

Preface

The Windows Azure™ technology platform offers exciting new opportunities for companies and developers to build large and complex applications to run in the cloud. Windows Azure enables you to take advantage of a pay-as-you-go billing model for your application infrastructure and on-demand computing resources.

By combining the existing Microsoft® Enterprise Library application blocks that help you design applications that are robust, configurable, and easy to manage, with new blocks designed specifically for the cloud, you can create highly scalable, robust applications that can take full advantage of Windows Azure.

This book describes a scenario based on a fictitious company named Tailspin that has decided to enhance its existing Windows Azure hosted application by using the new Autoscaling Application Block and Transient Fault Handling Block. Its Windows Azure-based application, named Surveys, is described in detail in a previous book in this series, "Developing Applications for the Cloud" at *http://msdn. microsoft.com/en-us/library/ff966499.aspx*.

This guide accompanies a reference implementation, which we encourage you to study and play with to better understand how the new application blocks operate.

In addition to describing the Windows Azure application and how it uses the Enterprise Library blocks, this book provides a description of the key features of the blocks and general guidance on how you can use them in your own applications.

The result is that, after reading this book, you will be familiar with how to incorporate the Autoscaling Application Block and the Transient Fault Handling Application Block in your Windows Azure applications.

Who This Book Is For

This book demonstrates how you can use the Enterprise Library Integration Pack for Windows Azure in an existing Windows Azure application to enhance the maintainability, manageability, scalability, stability, and extensibility of the application. The book is intended for any architect, developer, or information technology (IT) professional who designs, builds, or operates applications and services that are appropriate for the cloud and who wants to learn how to realize the benefits of using Enterprise Library in a cloud-based application. You should be familiar with Windows Azure, the Microsoft .NET Framework, Microsoft Visual Studio® development system, ASP.NET, and Microsoft Visual C#® to derive full benefit from reading this guide. The next two chapters offer overviews of Windows Azure and the Enterprise Library Integration Pack for Windows Azure to help you get started.

Why This Book Is Pertinent Now

In general, the cloud has become a viable option for making your applications accessible to a broad set of customers. You may have already built and deployed applications to Windows Azure using the tools available for Visual Studio and the Windows Azure SDK for .NET. Just as Enterprise Library has helped you to address common, crosscutting concerns, such as logging and exception management, in your on-premises applications, the Integration Pack and its associated guidance will help you address the crosscutting concerns common to many cloud applications. Some of these crosscutting concerns will be the same as those in your on-premises applications, such as exception management and caching; some will be different, such as auto-scaling to meet elastic demand. This book shows you how you can address these concerns in the context of a common scenario: enhancing an existing Windows Azure application.

How This Book Is Structured

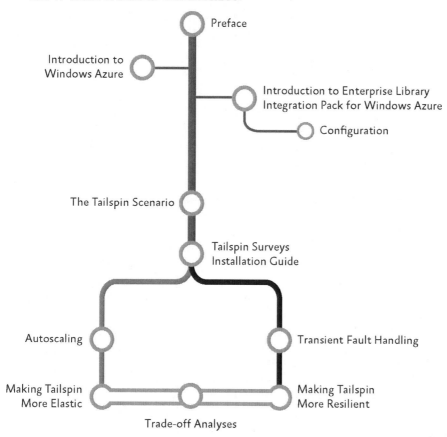

Preface

Introduction to Windows Azure

Introduction to Enterprise Library Integration Pack for Windows Azure

Configuration

The Tailspin Scenario

Tailspin Surveys Installation Guide

Autoscaling

Transient Fault Handling

Making Tailspin More Elastic

Making Tailspin More Resilient

Trade-off Analyses

What You Need to Use the Code

In order to run the Tailspin Surveys application, you will need the following:

- A development machine running Microsoft Visual Studio® 2010 development system SP1.

- All required Microsoft Windows® updates.

- NuGet Package Manager (for more information, see *http://nuget.codeplex.com/*).

- A Windows Azure subscription with room for two hosted services (if you want to run the Tailspin Surveys application, the Autoscaler Host, and the Management Web application in Windows Azure).

- A Windows Azure storage account.
- The Dependency Checker, which will verify that you have the prerequisites listed below installed. If not, it will help you install them.
- Visual Studio 2010
- MVC 3 Framework
- Windows Azure SDK for .NET and Windows Azure Tools for Microsoft Visual Studio – November 2011 Release
- Windows Identity Foundation Runtime
- Optional: Internet Information Services 7 (IIS) – This is required if you want to run the management site in simulated mode or want to deploy the autoscaler role locally.

Who's Who

As mentioned earlier, this book employs scenarios that demonstrate how to use the Enterprise Library Integration Pack for Windows Azure in a reference implementation. A panel of experts comments on the development efforts. The panel includes a cloud specialist, a business manager, a software architect, a software developer who is knowledgeable about Enterprise Library, a software developer who is new to Enterprise Library, and an IT professional. The scenarios can be considered from each of these points of view. The following table lists the experts for these scenarios.

Bharath is a cloud specialist. He checks that a cloud-based solution will work for a company and provide tangible benefits. He is a cautious person, for good reasons.

> Developing a single application to the cloud is easy. Realizing the benefits that a cloud-based solution can offer is not always so straightforward.

Jana is a software architect. She plans the overall structure of an application. Her perspective is both practical and strategic. In other words, she considers not only what technical approaches are needed today, but also what direction a company needs to consider for the future. Jana has worked on many projects that have used Enterprise Library.

> It's not easy to balance the needs of the company, the users, the IT organization, the developers, and the technical platforms we rely on.

Markus is a software developer who is new to Enterprise Library. He is analytical, detail-oriented, and methodical. He's focused on the task at hand, which is building a great cloud-based application. He knows that he's the person who's ultimately responsible for the code.

> I don't care what platform you want to use for the application, I'll make it work.

Ed is an experienced software developer and Enterprise Library expert. As a true professional, he is well aware of the common crosscutting concerns that developers face when building line-of-business (LOB) applications for the enterprise. In the past, he has built his own libraries to satisfy these concerns, but in the last several years he has used Enterprise Library for most of these applications.

> Our applications use Enterprise Library for crosscutting concerns. This provides a level of uniformity across all our systems that make them easier to support and maintain. We have invested heavily in our on premises applications and we must be able to reuse this investment in the cloud.

Poe is an IT professional who's an expert in deploying and running applications in the cloud. Poe has a keen interest in practical solutions; after all, he's the one who gets paged at 3:00 AM when there's a problem.

> Migrating applications in the cloud involves different challenges from managing on-premises applications. I want to make sure our cloud apps are as reliable and secure as our on-premise apps.

Beth is a business manager. She helps companies to plan how their business will develop. She understands the market that the company operates in, the resources that the company has available, and the goals of the company. She has both a strategic view, and an interest in the day-to-day operations of the company.

> Organizations face many conflicting demands on their resources. I want to make sure that our company balances those demands and adopts a business plan that will make us successful in the medium and long term.

If you have a particular area of interest, look for notes provided by the specialists whose interests align with yours.

Acknowledgments

THE TEAM WHO BROUGHT YOU THIS GUIDE

Authors	Dominic Betts, Jérémi Bourgault, Julian Dominguez, Ercenk Keresteci, Grigori Melnik, Fernando Simonazzi, and Erwin van der Valk
Technical Reviewers	Neil Mackenzie, Valery Mizonov, Eugenio Pace, Paweł Wilkosz, and Michael Wood
Book Designer	John Hubbard
Graphic Artist	Katie Niemer
Editors	RoAnn Corbisier, Nelly Delgado, and Nancy Michell

THE ENTERPRISE LIBRARY INTEGRATION PACK FOR WINDOWS AZURE DEVELOPMENT TEAM

Product/Program Management	Grigori Melnik (Microsoft Corporation)
Architecture/ Development	Julian Dominguez (Microsoft Corporation), Fernando Simonazzi (Clarius Consulting), Jérémi Bourgault (nVentive Inc.), and Ercenk Keresteci (Full Scale 180 Inc)
Testing	Mani Krishnaswami and Carlos Farre (Microsoft Corporation), Neeraj Jain, Murugesh Muthuvilavan, Karthick Natarajan, Thamilarasi Nataraj and Rathi Velusamy (Infosys Technologies Ltd.)
User Experience/ Documentation	Dominic Betts, Nancy Michell (Content Master Ltd.), Rick Carr (DCB Software Testing, Inc.), Nelly Delgado (Microsoft Corporation) and Erwin van der Valk (Erwin van der Valk)
Release Management	Richard Burte (ChannelCatalyst.com, Inc.), Grigori Melnik (Microsoft Corporation), and Jérémi Bourgault (nVentive Inc.)
Administrative Support	Kerstin Scott (Microsoft Corporation)

ADVISORS

Many people contributed to this release. We are grateful to all of them!

Advisory Council

Nikolai Blackie (Adaptiv), Ivan Bodyagin (ABBYY), Federico Boerr (Southworks), Leandro Boffi (Tellago), Michael Collier (Independent), Hans De Graaf (New Day at Work), Jason De Oliveira (Capgemini Sogeti), Dave Fellows (Green Button), Ştefan Filip (HPC Consulting), Sam Fold (Arkadium), Nuno Filipe Godinho (Independent), Neil Mackenzie (Independent), Daniel Piessens (Zywave), Marc Remmers (42windmills), Keith Stobie (Independent), François Tanguay (nVentive), Mihai Tataran (HPC Consulting), Stas Tkachenko (Arkadium), Trent Swenson (Full Scale 180), Gabriel Szletchman (3mellons), Philippe Vialatte (Independent), Guido Vilariño (3mellons/Disney), Oleg Volkov (New Day At Work), Paweł Wilkosz (Motorola Solution Systems), Michael Wood (Cumulux Inc.), and our Microsoft colleagues: Mark Aggar, David Aiken, Kashif Alam, Jaime Alva Bravo, Cihan Biyikoglu, Jim Davis, John Dawson, Scott Densmore, Lenny Fenster, Danny Garber, Rick Hines, Tom Hollander, Dmitri Martynov, Steve Marx, Tony Meleg, Suren Machiraju, Ade Miller, Valery Mizonov, Walter Myers, Masashi Narumoto, Bhushan Nene, Eugenio Pace, Curt Peterson, James Podgorski, Srilatha Rayasam, Paolo Salvatori, Marc Schweigert, Mark Simms, Eric Slippern, Vijay Sen, and Tim Wieman.

The contributions of Valery Mizonov and the whole AppFabric Customer Advisory Team (CAT) deserve a special mention. The Transient Fault Handling Application Block is based on the detection and retry strategies originally developed by the AppFabric CAT team. The enhanced Transient Fault Handling Application Block is a collaboration between the patterns & practices and the AppFabric CAT teams.

We'd also like to highlight our exceptional collaboration with Microsoft Consulting Services (Lenny Fenster, Danny Garber, Rick Hines, Walter Myers, and Marc Schweigert) whose regular feedback helped us stay grounded in the real world scenarios. Thank you for not letting us overlook many important ones.

COMMUNITY

Many thanks to Rahul Rai, Sudhakar Reddy D V, Maarten Baaliauw, Zoiner Tejada and all who voted on the backlog, beta tested our early code drops, and provided meaningful feedback. Also, we thank the attendees of the patterns & practices symposia, TechReady, and TechEd conferences who provided informal feedback.

1

Introduction to Windows Azure

This chapter provides a brief description of the Windows Azure™ technology platform, the services it provides, and the opportunities it offers for on-demand, cloud-based computing where the *cloud* is a set of interconnected computing resources located in one or more data centers. The chapter also provides links to help you find more information about the features of Windows Azure, the techniques and technologies used in this series of guides, and the sample code that accompanies them.

The primary purpose of this developer guide is to show how to use the Enterprise Library Integration Pack for Windows Azure with your Windows Azure applications. The accompanying reference implementation (sample demo), and the associated hands-on labs utilize many of the features and services available in Windows Azure, so it is useful to have an understanding of Windows Azure itself before you begin using the Enterprise Library Integration Pack for Windows Azure. If you are already familiar with Windows Azure, you can skip this chapter and move on to the chapters that describe the Enterprise Library Integration Pack for Windows Azure and the reference implementation, called the Tailspin Surveys application.

Windows Azure is a fast-moving platform, so for the very latest information about any of the features described in this chapter, you should follow the provided links.

About Windows Azure

Organizations can use the cloud to deploy and run applications and to store data. On-premises applications can use cloud-based resources as well. For example, an application located on an on-premises server, a rich client that runs on a desktop computer, or one that runs on a mobile device can use storage that is located on the cloud.

For more information about hybrid solutions, see the integration guide at *http://wag.codeplex.com/.*

Windows Azure abstracts hardware resources through virtualization. Each application that is deployed to Windows Azure runs on one or more virtual machines (VMs). These deployed applications behave

as though they were on a dedicated computer, although they might share physical resources such as disk space, network I/O, or CPU cores with other VMs on the same physical host. Two key benefits of an abstraction layer above the physical hardware are portability and scalability. Virtualizing a service allows it to be moved to any number of physical hosts in the data center. By combining virtualization technologies, commodity hardware, multi-tenancy, and aggregation of demand, Microsoft and our customers can achieve economies of scale. Such economies generate higher data center utilization (that is, more useful work-per-dollar hardware cost) and, subsequently, savings that are passed along to you.

Virtualization also allows you to have both *vertical scalability* and *horizontal scalability*. Vertical scalability means that, as demand increases, you can increase the number of resources, such as CPU cores or memory, on a specific VM. Horizontal scalability means that you can add more instances of VMs that are copies of existing services. All these instances are load balanced at the network level so that incoming requests are distributed among them.

At the time of this writing, Windows Azure encompasses Windows Azure and SQL Azure.

Windows Azure provides a Microsoft® Windows Server®-based computing environment for applications and persistent storage for both structured and unstructured data, as well as asynchronous messaging. Windows Azure also provides a range of services that helps you connect users and on-premises applications to cloud-hosted applications, manage authentication, use inter-service messaging, and implement data management and related features such as caching.

Windows Azure also includes a range of management services that allows you to control all these resources, either through a web-based user interface (a web portal) or programmatically. In most cases there is a REST-based API that can be used to define how your services will work. Most management tasks that can be performed through the web portal can also be performed using the API.

SQL Azure is essentially SQL Server® provided as a service in the cloud.

Finally, there is a comprehensive set of tools and software development kits (SDKs) that allow you to develop, test, and deploy your applications. For example, you can develop and test your applications in a simulated local environment, provided by the Compute Emulator and the Storage Emulator. Most tools are also integrated into development environments such as Microsoft Visual Studio® development system. In addition, there are third-party management tools available.

WINDOWS AZURE SERVICES AND FEATURES

The range of services and features available on Windows Azure and SQL Azure target specific requirements for your applications. When you subscribe to Windows Azure, you can choose which of the features you require, and you pay only for the features you use. You can add and remove features from your subscription whenever you wish. The billing mechanism for each service depends on the type of features the service provides. For more information on the billing model, see *"Windows Azure Subscription and Billing Model,"* later in this chapter.

The services and features available change as Windows Azure continues to evolve. The following four sections of this chapter briefly describe the main services and features available at the time of this writing, subdivided into the categories of Compute Environment, Data Management, Networking Services, and Other Services.

For more information about all of the Windows Azure services and features, see *"Windows Azure Features"* on the Windows Azure Portal. For specific development and usage guidance on each feature or service, see the resources referenced in the following sections.

Windows Azure includes a range of services that can simplify development, increase reliability, and make it easier to manage your cloud-hosted applications.

> *To use any of these features and services you must have a subscription to Windows Azure. A valid Windows Live® ID is required when signing up for a Windows Azure account. For more information, see "Windows Azure Offers."*

Compute Environment

The Windows Azure compute environment consists of a platform for applications and services hosted within one or more roles. The types of roles you can implement in Windows Azure are:

- **Windows Azure Compute (Web and Worker Roles).** A Windows Azure application consists of one or more hosted roles running within the Azure data centers. Typically there will be at least one web role that is exposed for access by users of the application. A web role is supported by Internet Information Service (IIS) 7.0 and ASP.NET. The application may contain additional roles, including worker roles, that are typically used to perform background processing and support tasks for web roles. For more detailed information, see *"Overview of Creating a Hosted Service for Windows Azure"* and *"Building an Application that Runs in a Hosted Service."*

- **Virtual Machine (VM role).** This role allows you to host your own custom instance of the Windows Server 2008 R2 Enterprise or Windows Server 2008 R2 Standard operating system within a Windows Azure data center. For more detailed information see *"Creating Applications by Using a VM Role in Windows Azure."*

The Tailspin Surveys application uses both web and worker roles. For additional information and guidance about the use of web and worker roles see the associated guides *"Moving Applications to the Cloud"* and *"Developing Applications for the Cloud"* which are available at *Cloud Development* on MSDN. Each of these guides also includes a set of hands-on labs.

Data Management

Windows Azure, SQL Azure, and the associated services provide opportunities for storing and managing data in a range of ways. The following data management services and features are available:

- **Windows Azure Storage**. This provides four core services for persistent and durable data storage in the cloud. The services support a REST interface that can be accessed from within Windows Azure-hosted or on-premises (remote) applications. For information about the REST API, see *"Windows Azure Storage Services REST API Reference."* The four storage services are listed below.

- **The Windows Azure Table Service** provides a table-structured storage mechanism and supports queries for managing the data. The Azure Table Service is a NoSQL offering that provides schema-less storage. It is primarily aimed at scenarios where large volumes of data must be stored, while being easy to access and update. For more detailed information see *"Table Service Concepts"* and *"Table Service REST API."*

- **The Binary Large Object (BLOB) Service** provides a series of containers aimed at storing text or binary data. It provides both Block BLOB containers for streaming data, and Page BLOB containers for random read/write operations. For more detailed information see *"Understanding Block Blobs and Page Blobs"* and *"Blob Service REST API."*

- **The Queue Service** provides a mechanism for reliable, persistent messaging between role instances, such as between a web role and a worker role. For more detailed information see *"Queue Service Concepts"* and *"Queue Service REST API."*

- **Windows Azure Drives** provide a mechanism for applications to mount a single volume NTFS VHD as a Page BLOB, and upload and download VHDs via the BLOB. For more detailed information see *"Windows Azure Drive."*

- **SQL Azure Database**. This is a highly available and scalable cloud database service built on SQL Server technologies, that supports the familiar T-SQL-based relational database model. It can be used with applications hosted in Windows Azure, and with other applications running on-premises or hosted elsewhere. For more detailed information see *"SQL Azure Database."*

- **Data Synchronization**. SQL Azure Data Sync is a cloud-based data synchronization service built on Microsoft Sync Framework technologies. It provides bi-directional data synchronization and data management capabilities, allowing data to be easily shared between multiple SQL Azure databases and between on-premises and SQL Azure databases. For more detailed information see *"Microsoft Sync Framework Developer Center."*

- **Caching**. This service provides a distributed, in-memory, low latency and high throughput application cache service that requires no installation or management, and dynamically increases and decreases the cache size as required. It can be used to cache application data, ASP.NET session state information, and for ASP.NET, page output caching. For more detailed information see *"Windows Azure Caching Service."*

The Tailspin Surveys application uses both Windows Azure storage and SQL Azure. For additional information and guidance about the use of Windows Azure storage and SQL Azure see the associated guides *"Moving Applications to the Cloud"* and *"Developing Applications for the Cloud"* which are available at *Cloud Development* on MSDN. Each of these guides also includes a set of hands-on labs.

Networking Services

Windows Azure provides several networking services that you can take advantage of to maximize performance, implement authentication, and improve manageability of your hosted applications. These services include the following:

- **Content Delivery Network (CDN)**. The CDN allows you to cache publicly available static data for applications at strategic locations that are closer (in network delivery terms) to end users. The CDN uses a number of data centers at many locations around the world, which store the data in BLOB storage that has anonymous access. These do not need to be locations where the application is actually running. For more detailed information see *"Delivering High-Bandwidth Content with the Windows Azure CDN."*

- **Virtual Network Connect**. This service allows you to configure roles of an application running in Windows Azure and computers on your on-premises network so that they appear to be on the same network. It uses a software agent running on the on-premises computer to establish an IPsec-protected connection to the Windows Azure roles in the cloud, and provides the capability to administer, manage, monitor, and debug the roles directly. For more detailed information see *"Connecting Local Computers to Windows Azure Roles."*

• **Virtual Network Traffic Manager**. This is a service that allows you to set up request redirection and load balancing based on three different techniques. Typically you will use Traffic Manager to maximize performance by using the Performance technique to redirect requests to the instance of your application in the data center closest to the user. Alternative load balancing methods available are Failover and Round Robin. For more detailed information see *"Windows Azure Traffic Manager."*

• **Access Control (ACS)**. This is a standards-based service for identity and access control that makes use of a range of identity providers (IdPs) that can authenticate users. ACS acts as a Security Token Service (STS), or token issuer, and makes it easier to take advantage of federation authentication techniques where user identity is validated in a realm or domain other than that in which the application resides. An example is controlling user access based on an identity verified by an identity provider such as Windows Live® ID or Google. For more detailed information see *"Access Control Service 2.0"* and *"A Guide to Claims-Based Identity and Access Control (2nd Edition)."*

• **Service Bus**. This provides a secure messaging and data flow capability for distributed and hybrid applications, such as communication between Windows Azure hosted applications and on-premises applications and services, without requiring complex firewall and security infrastructures. It can use a range of communication and messaging protocols and patterns to provide delivery assurance and reliable messaging, can scale to accommodate varying loads, and can be integrated with on-premises BizTalk Server artifacts. For more detailed information see *"Service Bus."*

For additional information and guidance about the use of Windows Azure storage and SQL Azure see the associated guides *"Moving Applications to the Cloud"* and *"Developing Applications for the Cloud"* which are available at *Cloud Development* on MSDN. Each of these guides also includes a set of hands-on labs.

Detailed guidance on using ACS can be found in the associated document, *"A Guide to Claims-Based Identity and Access Control (2nd Edition)"* and in the hands-on labs for that guide.

Other Services

Windows Azure provides the following additional services:

- **Business Intelligence Reporting**. This service allows you to develop and deploy to the cloud business operational reports generated from data stored in a SQL Azure database. It is built upon the same technologies as SQL Server Reporting Services, and lets you use familiar tools to generate reports. Reports can be easily accessed through the Windows Azure Management Portal, through a web browser, or directly from within your Windows Azure and on-premises applications. For more detailed information see *"SQL Azure Reporting."*

- **Marketplace**. This is an online facility where developers can share, find, buy, and sell building block components, training, service templates, premium data sets, and finished services and applications needed to build Windows Azure applications. For more detailed information see *"Windows Azure Marketplace"* on MSDN and *"Windows Azure Marketplace"* (AppMarket).

Developing Windows Azure Applications

Typically, on Microsoft® Windows®, you will use Visual Studio 2010 with the Windows Azure Tools for Microsoft Visual Studio. The Windows Azure Tools provide everything you need to create Windows Azure applications, including local compute and storage emulators that run on the development computer. This means that you can write, test, and debug applications before deploying them to the cloud. The tools also include features to help you deploy applications to Windows Azure and manage them after deployment.

You can download the Windows Azure Tools for Microsoft Visual Studio, and development tools for other platforms and languages such as iOS, Eclipse, Java, Ruby, and PHP from *"Windows Azure Tools."*

For a useful selection of videos, QuickStart examples, and hands-on labs that cover a range of topics to help you get started building Windows Azure applications, see *"Learn Windows Azure and SQL Azure"* and *"Design. Code. Scale."*

The MSDN *"Developing Applications for Windows Azure"* topic includes specific examples and guidance for creating hosted services, using the Windows Azure Tools for Microsoft Visual Studio to package and deploy applications, and a useful QuickStart example.

The *Windows Azure Training Kit* contains hands-on labs to get you started quickly.

To understand the execution lifecycle and how a Windows Azure role operates, see *"Real World: Startup Lifecycle of a Windows Azure Role."*

You can build and test Windows Azure applications using the compute and storage emulators on your development computer.

For a list of useful resources for developing and deploying data-bases in SQL Azure, see *"Development (SQL Azure Database)."*

For a list of tools that can help with planning the migration of an application to Windows Azure, see *"Planning and Designing Windows Azure Applications."*

Managing, Monitoring, and Debugging Windows Azure Applications

All storage and management subsystems in Windows Azure use REST-based interfaces. They are not dependent on any .NET Framework or Windows operating system technology. Any technology that can issue HTTP or HTTPS requests can access Windows Azure facilities.

To learn about the Windows Azure managed and native library APIs, and the storage services REST API, see *"API References for Windows Azure."*

The REST-based service management API can be used as an alternative to the Windows Azure web management portal. The API includes features to work with storage accounts, hosted services, certificates, affinity groups, locations, and subscription information. For more information, see *"Windows Azure Service Management REST API Reference."* In addition, Windows Azure provides diagnostic services and APIs for activities such as monitoring an application's health. You can use the Windows Azure Management Pack and System Center Operations Manager 2007 R2 to discover Windows Azure applications, get the status of each role instance, and collect and monitor performance information, Windows Azure events, and the .NET Framework trace messages from each role instance. For more information, see *"Monitoring Windows Azure Applications."*

Windows Azure includes features that allow you to monitor and debug cloud-hosted services.

You can also use the *Windows Azure PowerShell Cmdlets* to browse and manage Windows Azure compute and storage services, automate deployment, and upgrade your Windows Azure applications, as well as manage your diagnostics data.

For information about using the Windows Azure built-in trace objects to configure diagnostics and instrumentation without using Operations Manager, and about downloading the results, see *"Collecting Logging Data by Using Windows Azure Diagnostics."*

For information about debugging Windows Azure applications, see *"Troubleshooting and Debugging in Windows Azure"* and *"Debugging Applications in Windows Azure."*

> *Chapter 7, "Application Life Cycle Management for Windows Azure Applications" in the guide "Moving Applications to the Cloud" contains information about managing Windows Azure applications.*

Managing SQL Azure Databases

Applications access SQL Azure databases in exactly the same way they access locally installed SQL Server instances using the managed ADO.NET data access classes, Enterprise Library Data Access Application Block (DAAB), OData, native ODBC, PHP, Ruby, or JDBC data access technologies.

SQL Azure databases can be managed through the web portal, SQL Server Management Studio, Visual Studio 2010 database tools, and a range of other tools for activities such as moving and migrating data, as well as command-line tools for deployment and administration.

A database manager is also available to make it easier to work with SQL Azure databases. For more information see *"Management Portal for SQL Azure."* For a list of other tools, see *"Windows Azure Downloads."*

SQL Azure supports a management API as well as management through the web portal. For information about the SQL Azure management API see *"Management REST API Reference."*

Upgrading Windows Azure Applications

After you deploy an application to Windows Azure, you will need to update it as you change the role services in response to new requirements, code improvements, or to fix bugs. You can simply redeploy a service by suspending and then deleting it, and then deploy the new version. However, you can avoid application downtime by performing staged deployments (uploading a new package and swapping it with the existing production version), or by performing an in-place upgrade (uploading a new package and applying it to the running instances of the service).

For information about how you can perform service upgrades by uploading a new package and swapping it with the existing production version, see *"How to Deploy a Service Upgrade to Production by Swapping VIPs in Windows Azure."*

For information about how you can perform in-place upgrades, including details of how services are deployed into upgrade and fault domains and how this affects your upgrade options, see *"How to Perform In-Place Upgrades on a Hosted Service in Windows Azure."*

> *If you only need to change the configuration information for a service without deploying new code, you can use the web portal or the management API to edit the service configuration file or to upload a new configuration file.*

Windows Azure Subscription and Billing Model

To use Windows Azure, you first create a billing account by signing up for *Microsoft Online Services* or through the Windows Azure portal at *https://windows.azure.com/*. The Microsoft Online Services customer portal manages subscriptions to all Microsoft services. Windows Azure is one of these, but there are others such as Business Productivity Online, Windows Office Live Meeting, and Windows Intune™ software and services.

This section is based on the information publicly available at the time of this writing.

Every billing account has a single account owner who is identified with a Windows Live ID. The account owner can create and manage subscriptions, view billing information and usage data, and specify the service administrator(s) for each subscription.

Administrators manage the individual hosted services for a Windows Azure subscription using the Windows Azure portal at *https://windows.azure.com/*. A Windows Azure subscription can include one or more of the following:

- Hosted services, consisting of hosted roles and the instances within each role. Roles and instances may be stopped, in production, or in staging mode.
- Storage accounts, consisting of Table, BLOB, and Queue storage instances.
- CDN instances.
- SQL Azure databases and Data Sync service.
- SQL Azure Reporting Services instances.
- Access Control, Service Bus, and Cache service instances.
- Virtual Network Connect and Traffic Manager instances.

Figure 1 illustrates the Windows Azure billing configuration for a standard subscription.

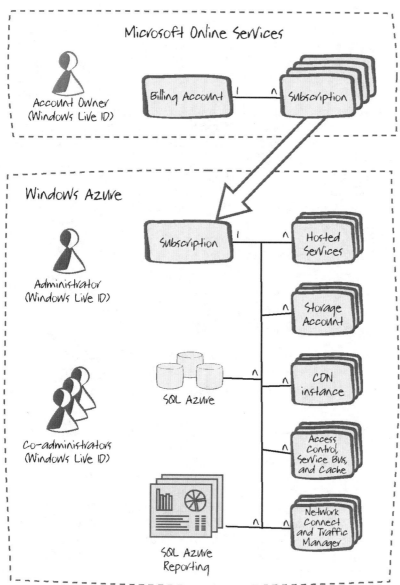

FIGURE 1
Windows Azure billing configuration for a standard subscription

For more information about Windows Azure billing, see *"What are the Billing Basics of Windows Azure?"* and *"Accounts and Billing in SQL Azure."*

You are billed for role resources that are used by a deployed service, even if the roles on those services are not running. If you don't want to get charged for a service, delete the deployments associated with the service.

Estimating Your Costs

Windows Azure charges are based on how you consume services such as compute time, storage, and bandwidth. Compute time charges are calculated on an hourly rate as well as a rate for the instance size. Storage charges are based on the number of gigabytes and the number of transactions. Prices for data transfer vary according to the geographic location you are in and generally apply to transfers between the Microsoft data centers and your premises, but not on transfers within the same data center.

To estimate the likely costs of a Windows Azure subscription, see the following resources:

* Subscription overview for the various purchasing models such as the pay-as-you-go and subscription model, including a tool for measuring consumption, at *http://www.microsoft.com/windowsazure/pricing/*.

* Pricing calculator at *http://www.microsoft.com/windowsazure/pricing-calculator/*.

* TCO calculator at *http://www.microsoft.com/windowsazure/offers/#tcoCompare-LB*.

> *Chapter 4, "How Much Will It Cost?" of the guide "Moving Applications to the Cloud" provides additional information about estimating the costs of hosting applications in Windows Azure.*

More Information

There is a great deal of information available about Windows Azure in the form of documentation, training videos, and white papers. Here are some websites you can visit to learn more:

* The portal to information about Windows Azure is at *http://www.microsoft.com/WindowsAzure/*. It has links to white papers, tools such as the Windows Azure SDK for .NET, and many other resources. You can also sign up for a Windows Azure account there.

* The Windows Azure learning portal at *http://www.microsoft.com/WindowsAzure/learn*.

* Wade Wegner and Steve Marx have a series of Channel 9 discussions about Windows Azure on Cloud Cover, located at *http://channel9.msdn.com/shows/Cloud+Cover/*.

* Find answers to your questions on the Windows Azure Forum at *http://social.msdn.microsoft.com/Forums/en-US/windowsazure-development/threads*

- Steve Marx is a Windows Azure Technical Product Manager. His blog is at *http://blog.smarx.com/*. It is a great source of news and information on Windows Azure.

- Wade Wegner is the Technical Evangelist Lead for Windows Azure. His blog is full of technical details and tips. It is at *http://www.wadewegner.com/*.

- Windows Azure Feature Voting backlog at *http://www.mygreatwindowsazureidea.com* to provide feedback, submit and vote on features requests.

- The community site for the patterns & practices series of guides at *http://wag.codeplex.com/* provides links to online resources, sample code, hands-on labs, feedback, and more.

- The community site for this release at *http://entlib.uservoice. com/forums/101257-windows-azure-integration-pack* provides links to additional online resources, issue tracker and discussion forum.

Below are the links to references in this chapter:

- Windows Azure Guidance on CodePlex:
  http://wag.codeplex.com/

- Windows Azure Features:
  http://www.microsoft.com/windowsazure/features/

- Windows Azure Offers:
  http://www.microsoft.com/windowsazure/offers/

- Overview of Creating a Hosted Service for Windows Azure:
  http://go.microsoft.com/fwlink/?LinkID=234572

- Building an Application that Runs in a Hosted Service:
  http://go.microsoft.com/fwlink/?LinkID=234587

- Creating Applications by Using a VM Role in Windows Azure:
  http://go.microsoft.com/fwlink/?LinkID=234590

- Cloud Development:
  http://go.microsoft.com/fwlink/?LinkID=234613

- Windows Azure Storage Services REST API Reference:
  http://msdn.microsoft.com/en-us/library/dd179355.aspx

- Table Service Concepts:
  http://msdn.microsoft.com/en-us/library/dd179463.aspx

- Table Service REST API:
  http://msdn.microsoft.com/en-us/library/dd179423.aspx

- Understanding Block Blobs and Page Blobs:
  http://msdn.microsoft.com/en-us/library/ee691964.aspx

- Blob Service REST API:
  http://msdn.microsoft.com/en-us/library/dd135733.aspx

- Queue Service Concepts:
  http://msdn.microsoft.com/en-us/library/dd179353.aspx
- Queue Service REST API:
  http://msdn.microsoft.com/en-us/library/dd179363.aspx
- Windows Azure Drive:
  http://go.microsoft.com/?linkid=9710117
- SQL Azure Database:
  http://msdn.microsoft.com/en-us/library/ee336279.aspx
- Microsoft Sync Framework Developer Center:
  http://msdn.microsoft.com/en-us/sync
- Caching Service (Windows Azure):
  http://go.microsoft.com/fwlink/?LinkID=234591
- Delivering High-Bandwidth Content with the Windows Azure CDN:
  http://go.microsoft.com/fwlink/?LinkID=234592
- Connecting Local Computers to Windows Azure Roles:
  http://go.microsoft.com/fwlink/?LinkID=234593
- Windows Azure Traffic Manager:
  http://go.microsoft.com/fwlink/?LinkID=234594
- Access Control Service 2.0:
  http://go.microsoft.com/fwlink/?LinkID=234595
- A Guide to Claims-Based Identity and Access Control (2nd Edition):
  http://msdn.microsoft.com/en-us/library/ff423674.aspx
- Service Bus:
  http://go.microsoft.com/fwlink/?LinkID=234596
- SQL Azure Reporting:
  http://go.microsoft.com/fwlink/?LinkID=234597
- Windows Azure Marketplace:
  http://go.microsoft.com/fwlink/?LinkID=234598
- Windows Azure Marketplace:
  http://go.microsoft.com/fwlink/?LinkID=234599
- Windows Azure Tools:
  http://www.microsoft.com/windowsazure/tools/
- Learn Windows Azure and SQL Azure:
  http://www.microsoft.com/windowsazure/tutorials/
- Design. Code. Scale.:
  http://www.microsoft.com/windowsazure/getstarted/
- Developing Applications for Windows Azure:
  http://go.microsoft.com/fwlink/?LinkID=234600

- Windows Azure Training Kit:
  http://go.microsoft.com/fwlink/?LinkID=234601
- Real World: Startup Lifecycle of a Windows Azure Role:
  http://go.microsoft.com/fwlink/?LinkID=234602
- Development (SQL Azure Database):
  http://go.microsoft.com/fwlink/?LinkID=234603
- Windows Azure Assessment/Planning:
  http://www.microsoft.com/windowsazure/tools/#assessment
- API References for Windows Azure:
  http://msdn.microsoft.com/en-us/library/ff800682.aspx
- Windows Azure Service Management REST API Reference:
  http://msdn.microsoft.com/en-us/library/ee460799.aspx
- Monitoring Windows Azure Applications:
  http://msdn.microsoft.com/en-us/library/gg676009.aspx
- Windows Azure PowerShell Cmdlets:
  http://wappowershell.codeplex.com/
- Collecting Logging Data by Using Windows Azure Diagnostics:
  http://go.microsoft.com/fwlink/?LinkID=234604
- Troubleshooting and Debugging in Windows Azure:
  http://go.microsoft.com/fwlink/?LinkID=234605
- Debugging Applications in Windows Azure:
  http://go.microsoft.com/fwlink/?LinkID=234606
- "Application Life Cycle Management for Windows Azure
  Applications" in Moving Applications to the Cloud:
  http://msdn.microsoft.com/en-us/library/ff803362.aspx
- Management Portal for SQL Azure:
  http://go.microsoft.com/fwlink/?LinkID=234607
- Windows Azure Tools:
  http://www.microsoft.com/windowsazure/tools/#sqlazure
- Management REST API Reference:
  http://go.microsoft.com/fwlink/?LinkID=234608
- How to Deploy a Service Upgrade to Production by Swapping
  VIPs in Windows Azure:
  http://go.microsoft.com/fwlink/?LinkID=234609
- How to Perform In-Place Upgrades on a Hosted Service in
  Windows Azure:
  http://go.microsoft.com/fwlink/?LinkID=234610
- Microsoft Online Services:
  https://mocp.microsoftonline.com/

- "What are the Billing Basics of Windows Azure?" in "Windows Azure Platform"
  http://go.microsoft.com/fwlink/?LinkID=234611
- Accounts and Billing in SQL Azure:
  http://go.microsoft.com/fwlink/?LinkID=234612
- Subscription overview for the various purchasing models:
  http://www.microsoft.com/windowsazure/pricing/
- Pricing calculator:
  http://www.microsoft.com/windowsazure/pricing-calculator/
- TCO calculator:
  http://www.microsoft.com/windowsazure/offers/#tcoCompare-LB
- "How Much Will It Cost?" in Moving Applications to the Cloud:
  http://msdn.microsoft.com/en-us/library/ff803375.aspx
- Moving Applications to the Cloud, 2nd Edition:
  http://msdn.microsoft.com/en-us/library/ff728592.aspx

To access web resources more easily, see the online version of the bibliography on MSDN:
http://msdn.microsoft.com/en-us/library/hh749032(v=PandP.50).aspx

2   Introduction to Enterprise Library Integration Pack for Windows Azure

The Microsoft® Enterprise Library Integration Pack for Windows Azure extends Enterprise Library to include support for Windows Azure™ technology platform applications. It includes additional application blocks to meet the requirements of cloud-hosted applications.

What Is Enterprise Library?

Enterprise Library provides many highly configurable features that make it much easier for you to manage the repetitive tasks, known as crosscutting concerns, which occur in many places in your applications. These tasks include logging, validation, caching, exception management, and more. In addition, the dependency injection container provided by Enterprise Library can help you to simplify and decouple your designs, make them more testable and understandable, and help you to produce more efficient designs and implementations of all kinds of applications.

Enterprise Library consists of a collection of application blocks and a core infrastructure. All of these are reusable software components designed to assist developers with common enterprise development challenges. Each application block is designed to address a specific set of concerns. For example, the Logging Application Block simplifies the implementation of common logging functions in your application and enables you to write logging information to a variety of locations; the Data Access Application Block simplifies the development of common data access tasks such as reading data for display in a UI or submitting changed data back to the underlying database system.

As shown in Figure 1, the application blocks in Enterprise Library are:

- *The Caching Application Block*. You can use this application block to incorporate a local cache into your applications.

- *The Cryptography Application Block*. This application block can be used to incorporate hashing and symmetric encryption into your applications.

- *The Data Access Application Block*. Use this application block to incorporate standard database functionality into your applications.

- *The Exception Handling Application Block*. Developers and policy makers can use this application block to create a consistent strategy for processing exceptions that occur throughout the architectural layers of enterprise applications.

- *The Logging Application Block*. Developers can use this application block to include standard logging functionality in their applications and systems administrators can use the configuration tool to adjust the granularity of logging at run time.

- *The Policy Injection Application Block*. This block contains legacy code for backwards compatibility with existing applications. The new functionality is available by using the Unity interception mechanism and call handlers located in the related application block assemblies.

- *The Security Application Block*. Developers can use this application block to incorporate authorization and security caching functionality into their applications.

- *The Validation Application Block*. Developers can use this application block to create validation rules for business objects that can be used across different layers of their applications.

- *Unity Dependency Injection and Interception*. Developers can use these techniques to implement a lightweight, extensible dependency injection container with support for constructor, property, and method call injection, and to capture calls to target objects and add additional functionality to the object.

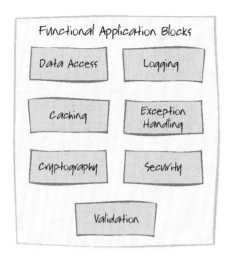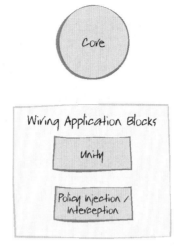

FIGURE 1
Enterprise Library components

Enterprise Library is configuration-driven and supports both pro-grammatic and external configuration. As well as the application blocks, Enterprise Library contains configuration tools, plus a set of core functions that manage tasks applicable to all of the blocks.

The goals of Enterprise Library are the following:

- **Consistency**. All Enterprise Library application blocks feature consistent design patterns and implementation approaches.

- **Extensibility**. All application blocks include defined extensibility points that allow developers to customize the behavior of the blocks by adding their own code.

- **Ease of use**. Enterprise Library offers numerous usability benefits, including a graphical configuration tool, a simple installation procedure, and clear and complete documentation and samples.

- **Integration**. Enterprise Library application blocks are designed to work well together and are tested to make sure that they do. However, you do not have to use them together.

To learn more about Enterprise Library and the application blocks, visit the main Enterprise Library site on MSDN® at *Enterprise Library 5.0 – May 2011*.

What Is the Enterprise Library Integration Pack for Windows Azure?

The Enterprise Library Integration Pack for Windows Azure extends Enterprise Library 5.0 to add additional support for developing and managing Windows Azure applications. It shares the same benefits as the Enterprise Library and helps developers achieve the same goals.

The Enterprise Library Integration Pack for Windows Azure includes:

- The *Autoscaling Application Block* to help you to automatically scale your Windows Azure applications.
- The *Transient Fault Handling Application Block* to help you make your Windows Azure applications more resilient when they encounter transient fault conditions.
- The Blob configuration source to store your Enterprise Library configuration in Azure blob storage.
- A protected configuration provider.
- Windows PowerShell® command line interface cmdlets to manipulate the Autoscaling Application Block.
- Updated database creation scripts (for the Logging Application Block and Caching Application Block) to use SQL Azure™ technology platform.
- Reference documentation.
- A developer's guide.
- A reference implementation that illustrates the use of the new application blocks.

The Enterprise Library Integration Pack for Windows Azure is one of several existing and planned integration packs for Enterprise Library.

For more information about Enterprise Library, see *Microsoft Enterprise Library 5.0 – May 2011 and the Developer's Guide*.

For more information about the Silverlight Integration Pack for use with Microsoft Silverlight® browser plug-in applications, see *Enterprise Library 5.0 Silverlight Integration Pack*.

More Information

For more information about the Enterprise Library application blocks, see the following resources on MSDN:

- Microsoft Enterprise Library 5.0 – May 2011:
  http://msdn.microsoft.com/en-us/library/ff632023.aspx
- Developer's Guide:
  http://msdn.microsoft.com/en-us/library/ff953181(v=PandP.50).aspx
- Enterprise Library 5.0 Silverlight Integration Pack:
  http://entlib.codeplex.com/wikipage?title=EntLib5Silverlight
- The Caching Application Block:
  http://msdn.microsoft.com/en-gb/library/ff664753(PandP.50).aspx
- The Cryptography Application Block:
  http://msdn.microsoft.com/en-gb/library/ff664484(PandP.50).aspx
- The Data Access Application Block:
  http://msdn.microsoft.com/en-gb/library/ff664408(PandP.50).aspx
- The Exception Handling Application Block:
  http://msdn.microsoft.com/en-gb/library/ff664698(PandP.50).aspx
- The Logging Application Block:
  http://msdn.microsoft.com/en-gb/library/ff664569(PandP.50).aspx
- The Policy Injection Application Block:
  http://msdn.microsoft.com/en-gb/library/ff664572(PandP.50).aspx
- The Security Application Block:
  http://msdn.microsoft.com/en-gb/library/ff664771(PandP.50).aspx
- The Validation Application Block:
  http://msdn.microsoft.com/en-gb/library/ff664356(PandP.50).aspx
- Unity Dependency Injection and Interception:
  http://msdn.microsoft.com/unity

For more information about the Autoscaling Application Block, see "The Autoscaling Application Block" on MSDN:
http://msdn.microsoft.com/en-us/library/hh680892(v=PandP.50).aspx

For more information about the Transient Fault Handling Application Block, see "The Transient Fault Handling Application Block" on MSDN:
http://msdn.microsoft.com/en-us/library/hh680934(v=PandP.50).aspx

To access web resources more easily, see the online version of the bibliography on MSDN:
http://msdn.microsoft.com/en-us/library/hh749032(v=PandP.50).aspx

3   The Tailspin Scenario

This chapter introduces a fictitious company named **Tailspin**. It describes Tailspin's plan to use Microsoft Enterprise Library to further develop its flagship online service named **Surveys**. Surveys is a cloud-based service, hosted on the Windows Azure™ technology platform, that enables other companies or individuals to conduct their own online surveys and analyze the results. As with any company planning to update one of its key applications, there are many issues to consider and challenges to meet, particularly because this is the first time the developers at Tailspin have used Enterprise Library. The chapters that follow this one describe the benefits to Tailspin of using Enterprise Library and show, step by step, how Tailspin modified and re-architected the Surveys application to use Enterprise Library.

The Tailspin Company

Tailspin is a startup ISV company of approximately 20 employees that specializes in developing cloud solutions using Microsoft® technologies. The developers at Tailspin are knowledgeable about various Microsoft products and technologies, including Windows Azure, the .NET Framework, ASP.NET MVC, SQL Server®, and Microsoft Visual Studio® development system. These developers are aware of the capabilities of Enterprise Library, but have not yet incorporated it into any of their cloud-based applications.

The Surveys application was the first of several innovative online services that Tailspin took to market. As a startup, Tailspin decided to specialize in cloud-hosted solutions in order to minimize its hardware investments and maximize its ability to reach a global audience. Tailspin hoped that some of these cloud-hosted services would grow rapidly, and the company wanted to have the ability to respond quickly to increasing demand. Similarly, it fully expects some of these cloud-based services to fail, and it does not want to be left with redundant hardware on its hands. The Surveys application has been a major success for Tailspin, with thousands of existing customers around the world, and new customers signing up every day.

TAILSPIN'S STRATEGY

Tailspin is an innovative and agile organization, well placed to exploit new technologies and the business opportunities offered by the cloud. Tailspin's strategy has been to embrace the cloud and gain a competitive advantage as an early adopter, rapidly gaining some experience, and then quickly expanding on what it has learned. This strategy can be described as "try, fail fast, learn, and then try again." The Surveys application has been a huge commercial success for Tailspin, but its success has revealed some problems with the initial implementation in terms of its flexibility, manageability, and maintainability.

THE SURVEYS APPLICATION

The Surveys application enables Tailspin's customers to design a survey, publish it, and collect the results for analysis. A survey is a collection of questions, each of which can be one of several types, such as multiple choice, numeric range, or free text. Customers begin by creating a subscription with the Surveys service, which they use to manage their surveys and to apply branding by using styles and logo images. Customers can also select a geographic location for their account, so that they can host their surveys as close as possible to the survey audience. The Surveys application allows users to try out the application for free, and to sign up for one of several different packages that offer different collections of services for a monthly fee.

Figure 1 illustrates the Surveys application and highlights the three different groups of users (customers, Tailspin administrators, and Surveys participants) who interact with it.

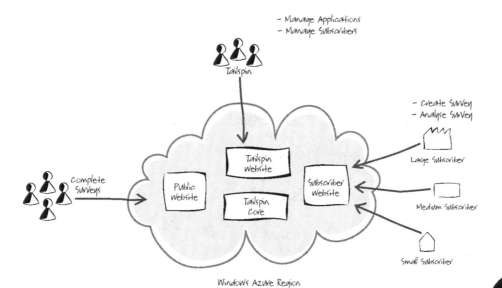

FIGURE 1
The Surveys application

Customers who have subscribed to the Surveys service (or who are using a free trial) access the Subscriber website, which enables them to design their own surveys, apply branding and customization, and collect and analyze the survey results. Depending on the package they select, they have access to different levels of functionality within the Surveys application. Tailspin expects its customers to be of various sizes and from all over the world, and customers can select a geographic location for their account and surveys.

Tailspin wants to design the service in such a way that most of the administrative and configuration tasks are "self-service" and can be performed by the subscriber with minimal intervention by Tailspin staff.

The public website enables the people participating in the survey to complete their responses to the survey questions. The survey creator will let their survey audience know what URL to visit to complete the survey.

The Tailspin website enables staff at Tailspin to manage the application and manage the subscriber accounts. All three websites (Subscriber, Public, and Tailspin) interact with the core services that comprise the Surveys application and provide access to the application's data storage.

> In the world of Software as a Service (SaaS), subscribers are commonly known as "Tenants." We commonly refer to applications like Tailspin Surveys as "multi-tenant" applications.

TAILSPIN'S GOALS AND CONCERNS

Tailspin faces several challenges with the current version of the Surveys application. The initial development was done quickly in order to be early to market. This resulted in some compromises during the development process whereby some features were sacrificed, and the design process was tailored to meet tight deadlines, not to optimize maintainability and extensibility. Tailspin sees this next phase in the life of the Surveys application as a consolidation phase that will lay the groundwork for the future development of the application and address the shortcomings of the initial implementation.

Here is how the original application works. First, customers create surveys. These might be associated with product launches or marketing campaigns, or they might be seasonal, perhaps associated with a holiday period. Often, customers who use the survey application set up these surveys with a very short lead time. Surveys usually run for a fixed, short period of time but may have a large number of respondents. This means that the Surveys application experiences bursts of usage, and Tailspin has very little warning of when these bursts occur. Tailspin now offers the Surveys application to customers around the world, and because the nature of the Surveys application includes sudden bursts in demand, it must be able to quickly expand or contract its infrastructure in different geographical locations. Up until now, Tailspin has relied on a process that requires an operator to manually add and remove role instances based on performance data collected from the application or in anticipation of known or planned events. In order to better serve its increasing number of customers and to control its costs, Tailspin would like to automate the scaling process.

Resource elasticity and geo-distribution are key properties of the Windows Azure platform.

The subscriber and public websites also have different scalability requirements. Thousands of users might complete a survey, but only a handful of users from each subscriber will edit existing surveys or create new surveys. Tailspin wants to optimize the resources for each of these scenarios.

When problems occur in the Surveys application, Tailspin sometimes struggles to resolve them quickly enough to meet its service-level agreements (SLA). Tailspin wants to be able to respond to issues and problems with the Surveys application more effectively by having better diagnostics data that is easily accessible.

Tailspin wants to be able to maintain its competitive advantage by rapidly rolling out new features to existing services or gain competitive advantage by being first to market with new products and services. For the Surveys application, Tailspin wants a platform with a clear, consistent architecture that is easy to extend and enhance.

The Tailspin business model is to charge subscribers a monthly fee for a service such as the Surveys application and, because of the global market they are operating in, Tailspin wants its prices to be competitive. Tailspin must then pay the actual costs of running the application, so in order to maintain their profit margin Tailspin must tightly control the running costs of the services they offer to their customers.

> In this scenario, Tailspin's customers (the subscribers) are **not** Windows Azure customers. Subscribers pay Tailspin, who in turn pays Microsoft for their use of Windows Azure features.

Tailspin wants to ensure that customer's data is kept safe. For example, a customer's data must be private to that customer, there must be multiple physical copies of the survey data, and customers should not be able to lose data by accidently deleting a survey. In addition, all existing survey data must be preserved whenever Tailspin updates the application.

As the number of subscribers grows, Tailspin wants to improve the resilience of the Surveys application to ensure that it can continue to meet its SLAs. This is particularly important for some of Tailspin's larger customers.

Finally, Tailspin would like to be able to leverage the existing skills of its developers, minimize any retraining necessary to build the Surveys application, and make it easy for developers to leverage the experience they have gained working on the Surveys application in Tailspin's other products.

The Surveys Application Architecture

To achieve the goals of the Surveys application, Tailspin implemented the application as a cloud-based service using Windows Azure. Figure 2 shows a high-level view of this architecture.

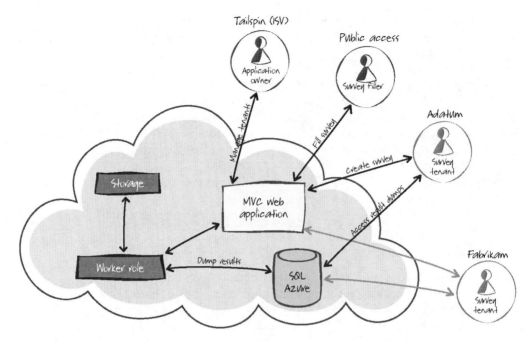

FIGURE 2
The Surveys application architecture

The architecture of the Surveys Application is straightforward and one that many other Windows Azure applications use. The core of the application uses Windows Azure web roles, worker roles, and storage. Figure 2 shows the three groups of users who access the application: the application owner, the public, and subscribers to the Surveys service (in this example, Adatum and Fabrikam). It also highlights how the application uses SQL Azure™ technology platform to provide a mechanism for subscribers to dump their survey results into a relational database to analyze the results in detail.

This guide discusses aspects of the design and implementation in detail and describes how the various web and worker roles that comprise the Surveys application make use of the Enterprise Library application blocks and services.

Some of the specific issues that the guide covers include how Tailspin implemented an autoscaling feature that enables the application to automatically scale up and scale down by adding and removing role instances and how Tailspin improved the resilience of the Surveys application to transient fault conditions.

Tailspin built the Surveys application using the latest available technologies: Visual Studio 2010, ASP.NET MVC 3.0, and .NET Framework 4.

More Information

For information about building a Windows Phone 7 client application for the Tailspin Surveys application, see the book, *Windows Phone 7 Developer Guide* at *http://go.microsoft.com/fwlink/?LinkID=234571*

4 Autoscaling and Windows Azure

What is Autoscaling?

One of the key benefits that the Windows Azure™ technology platform delivers is the ability to rapidly scale your application in the cloud in response to changes in demand.

When you deploy an application to Windows Azure, you deploy roles: web roles for the externally facing portions of your application and worker roles to handle back-end processing. When you run your application in Windows Azure, your roles run as role instances (you can think of role instances as virtual machines). You can specify how many role instances you want for each of your roles; the more instances you have, the more computing power you have available for that role, but the more it will cost you. There are, of course, some specific design requirements if your roles are to operate correctly when there are multiple instances of that role, but Windows Azure looks after the infrastructure requirements for you. For more information about design requirements, see *"Building a Scalable, Multi-Tenant Application for Windows Azure."*

You can specify the size and the number of instances you require for each of your roles when you first deploy an application to Windows Azure. You can also add or remove role instances on the fly while the application is running, either manually through the Windows Azure portal, or programmatically by using the Windows Azure Management API.

By adding and removing role instances to your Windows Azure application while it is running, you can balance the performance of the application against its running costs. You can add new instances when demand is high, and remove instances when you no longer need them in order to reduce running costs.

If you rely on manual interventions to scale your application, you may not always achieve the optimal balance between costs and performance; an operator may respond late, or underestimate the number of role instances that you need to maintain throughput.

Scalability is a key feature of the Windows Azure platform.

Scaling by adding additional instances is often referred to as *scaling out*. Windows Azure also supports *scaling up* by using larger role instances instead of more role instances.

31

You also need to consider the cost of having human operators performing this task, especially if you have hundreds or even thousands of role instances running in Windows Azure data centers around the globe.

You should evaluate your autoscaling behavior on a regular basis. Even with autoscaling in place, fire-and-forget is not the best practice.

The Autoscaling Application Block shares with other Enterprise Library blocks many design features, such as how you configure it and use it in your code.

An autoscaling solution reduces the amount of manual work involved in dynamically scaling an application. It can do this in two different ways: either preemptively by setting constraints on the number of role instances based on a timetable, or reactively by adjusting the number of role instances in response to some counter(s) or measurement(s) that you can collect from your application or from the Windows Azure environment.

You will still need to evaluate the results of your autoscaling solution on a regular basis to ensure that it is delivering the optimal balance between costs and performance. Your environment is unlikely to be static; overall, the numbers of users can change, access patterns by users can change, your application may perform differently as it stores more data, or you may deploy your application to additional Windows Azure data centers.

Scaling your application by adjusting the number of role instances may not be the best or only way to scale your application. For example, you may want to modify the behavior of your application in some way during bursts in demand, or to alter the number of Windows Azure queues, or the size of your SQL Azure database. An autoscaling solution may not be limited to just adjusting the number of role instances.

What is the Autoscaling Application Block?

The Autoscaling Application Block ("WASABi") is a part of the Enterprise Library Integration Pack for Windows Azure.

The application block allows you to define how your Windows Azure Application can automatically handle changes in the load levels that it might experience over time. It helps you minimize your operational costs, while still providing excellent performance and availability to your users. It also helps to reduce the number of manual tasks that your operators must perform.

The application block works through a collection of user-defined rules, which control when and how your application should respond when the load varies. Rules are either *constraint rules* that set limits on the minimum and maximum number of role instances in your Windows Azure application, or *reactive rules* that adjust the current number of role instances based on counters or measurements that you collect from your application.

Constraint rules can have an associated timetable that specifies the times when the rule is active. Constraint rules enable you to pro-actively set the number of role instances that your application can use; the minimum number of role instances helps you to meet your service level agreement (SLA) commitments, the maximum number of role instances helps you to control the running costs of your Windows Azure application.

Reactive rules use values that are derived either from system metrics such as CPU utilization, or from business metrics such as the number of unprocessed documents in the application. The application block collects these metrics and saves them as data points. A data point is simply the value of a metric with an associated timestamp to indicate when the application block collected the value. A reactive rule uses an aggregate value (such as average, maximum, minimum, or last) calculated from data points over a specified period. A reactive rule compares the current aggregate value to a threshold value, and based on the result performs one or more actions; for example, adding two new web role instances and notifying an operator. Reactive rules help your application respond to unexpected bursts (or collapses) in your application's workload.

Rules are stored in XML documents. This makes them easy to edit. It also makes it possible to build custom editors for the rules in your application. The Tailspin Surveys application shows how this can be done.

The Autoscaling Application Block supports the following techniques for handling varying load levels:

- **Instance Scaling**. The Autoscaling Application Block varies the number of role instances to accommodate variations in the load on the application.

- **Throttling**. The Autoscaling Application Block limits or disables certain (relatively) expensive operations in your application when the load is above certain thresholds.

These two autoscaling techniques are not mutually exclusive, and you can use both to implement a hybrid autoscaling solution in your application.

Figure 1 shows the relationship between the Autoscaling Application Block and your Windows Azure application.

In Windows Azure, changing the number of role instances takes time, so to respond quickly you may want to throttle your application until the new role instances are available.

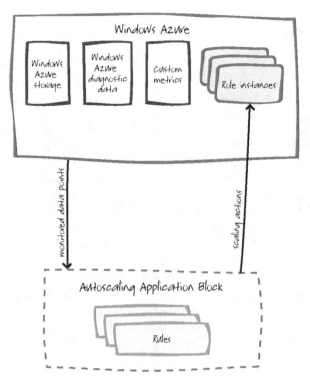

FIGURE 1
The Autoscaling Application Block and Windows Azure

This diagram illustrates how the Autoscaling Application Block collects data from your Windows Azure environment and uses that data in rules to determine if it should initiate any scaling actions in your Windows Azure application.

The Autoscaling Application Block can be hosted either in Windows Azure or on premises.

INSTANCE AUTOSCALING

The Autoscaling Application Block allows you to automatically scale out the number of Windows Azure role instances (web and worker roles) to closely match the demands of your application. This is an effective technique for controlling the running costs of your application, because in Windows Azure, you only pay for instances that you actually use.

Of course, it is important to set explicit boundaries for the autoscaling behavior in your Windows Azure application. Because you are billed for each provisioned role instance (regardless whether running or stopped), you must set a maximum number of instances for each

It's important to control the costs of running the application, keeping the number of role instances to a minimum helps us achieve that goal.

role type in your application. Otherwise, an application error that causes your number of role instances to increase could result in a significant (and unexpected) cost at the end of the month. You can also set a minimum number of role instances to ensure that your application runs and is resilient in the face of any failures.

> *You must have a minimum of two role instances to be eligible for the Windows Azure SLA guarantees.*

You shouldn't expect the Autoscaling Application Block to be able to start new role instances instantaneously; it takes Windows Azure a finite time to launch (or terminate) a role instance. The time taken is typically in the order of 10 minutes (at the time of writing this guide), but this can vary depending on a number of factors; for example, the number of role instances you are adding, the size of the role instances you are adding, and the current level of activity within the Windows Azure data center.

> *At the time of this writing, partial compute instance hours are billed as full compute hours for each clock hour an instance is deployed. For example, if you deploy a Small compute instance at 10:50 and delete the deployment at 11:10, then you will be billed for two Small compute hours, one compute hour for usage during 10:50 to 11:00 and another compute hour for usage during 11:00 to 11:10. Therefore, it makes sense to keep new instances alive for the remainder of the clock hour during which they were started. For more information, see* "**Usage Charge Details for Windows Azure Bills.**"
>
> *The stabilizer takes this into account for reactive rules (explained below), but you should consider designing your constraint rules (also explained below) so that they scale down just before the end of the clock hour.*

> It's important to choose carefully what you throttle. Users will expect the core functionality of your application to be available at all times.

APPLICATION THROTTLING

Instead of adjusting the number of role instances in response to changes in demand, you can use the Autoscaling Application Block to change the way your application behaves under various conditions. This technique allows you to specify modes of operation that are appropriate to certain load levels or times of day or user type.

For example, you can define different modes of operation for normal operation, for when there is very little load on your application, or for extreme bursts in activity.

- When the load on your application is very low, you might want to perform certain background processing tasks that are not time critical, but that might be resource intensive, such as exporting data or calculating statistics. If your SLA requires you

Depending on the size and complexity of your application, throttling may not happen faster than adding a new instance. Therefore, you must test it in your environment. You should also remember that not all of your instances will react to throttling at the same time.

to have a minimum of two instances to run your application, then you can use this technique to better utilize these instances by occupying them with background processing tasks.

- Under normal load, you might want to avoid executing background tasks, but otherwise run your application as normal.
- When an extreme burst in activity occurs, you might want to disable certain functionality so that your application remains usable. For example, you can disable autocomplete functionality, switch to a lightweight version of your user interface or disable some functionality for trial users while still providing full support for paying customers.

You can use application throttling very effectively in combination with instance scaling. It can take up to 10 minutes for Windows Azure to add a new role instance, so when a sudden burst of activity occurs, you can use application throttling to help reduce the load on your application while the new role instances start. However, if you have a large number of instances, it can take time for the configuration change to propagate to all the instances, by which time your new instances may have started. In addition, if your application is already scaled to the maximum number of role instances permitted by your constraint rules, then application throttling can help to provide the maximum performance for the core functionality in your application.

RULES AND ACTIONS

The Autoscaling Application Block uses rules and actions to determine how your application should respond to changes in demand. As described earlier, there are two types of rules: constraint rules and reactive rules, each with their own actions.

Constraint Rules

For many applications, the load pattern is predictable. For example, in a business application, the highest load is during office hours; on a consumer website, the highest load is between 18:00 and 20:00. In these scenarios, you can proactively scale your Windows Azure application to meet the anticipated additional workload. You can use constraint rules to address this scenario.

Constraint rules consist of one or more actions to set minimum and maximum values for the number of instances of a target, a rank, and optionally a timetable that defines when the rule is in effect. If there is no timetable, the rule is always in effect.

You can use a timetable to control the number of role instances that should be available at particular times. For example, you could

You should set the minimum value to ensure that you continue to meet your SLAs. You should set the maximum value to limit your costs and meet your budgetary goals.

create a rule to increase the minimum and maximum number of web and worker role instances in your application between 9:00 and 11:00 on Monday mornings when you know that demand for your application will be higher than usual.

You can also specify default rules that are always active and that specify default maximum and minimum values for the number of role instances for each web and worker role type in your application. Importantly, **constraint rules always take precedence over reactive rules**, to ensure that these reactive rules cannot continue to add new role instances above a maximum value or remove role instances below a minimum level.

> *By default (at the time of this writing), Windows Azure subscriptions are permitted to use up to 20 CPU cores. This value can be increased on request. For more information, see the* **Windows Azure Support** *page.*

It is possible that multiple constraint rules are in effect at the same time because of overlapping times in their timetables. In this case, the Autoscaling Application Block uses the *rank* of the rules to determine which rule takes precedence. Higher-ranked rules override lower ranked rules.

Here are some examples of constraint rules:

- For web role A, the default minimum number of instances is set to two and the maximum to four. This rule uses the default rank.

- On relatively busy Fridays, the minimum number of instances is set to four and the maximum to eight for web role A. This rule uses a higher rank.

- For worker role B, the default constraint is a minimum of two instances and a maximum of four instances.

- On Saturdays and Sundays between 2:00 PM and 6:00 PM, for worker role B, set the minimum number of instances to three and the maximum to six.

- On the last Friday of every month, for scale group A, set the minimum number of instances to three and the maximum to six (scale groups are described later in this chapter).

Figure 2 illustrates the behavior of the Autoscaling Application Block when you have multiple constraint rules defined. The scenario displayed in the diagram uses three separate constraint rules to determine the number of instances of worker role A in your application. There are no reactive rules in this simple scenario.

One is the lowest rank. You should use it for all your default rules. You should always assign a rank to your constraint rules so that it's clear which one should take precedence.

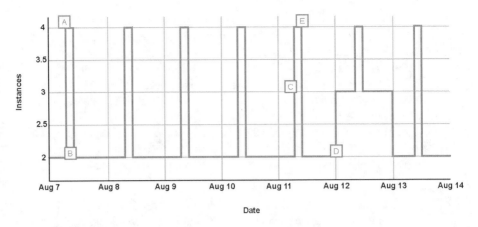

FIGURE 2
Using multiple constraint rules and no reactive rules

The three constraint rules in effect in this scenario work as follows:

1. The first constraint rule is always active. It sets the maximum and minimum number of instances for worker role A to two. This rule has the lowest rank.

2. The second constraint rule is active between 8:00 AM and 10:00 AM every day. In the diagram, label A shows when this rule became active on August 7, and label B shows when this rule became inactive. It sets the maximum and minimum number of instances for worker role A to four. It has the highest rank of the three rules, so when it overlaps with any other rules it takes precedence.

3. The third constraint rule is active every Friday (in the diagram, 12 August is a Friday, and labels C and D show when this rule became active and inactive). It sets the maximum and minimum number of instances for worker role A to three. It has a lower rank than the second rule, so between 8:00 AM and 10:00 AM on Fridays, the second rule overrides this rule; in the diagram, label E shows when this happened.

Figure 3 shows the effect of using multiple constraint rules with different maximum and minimum values, but without any reactive rules.

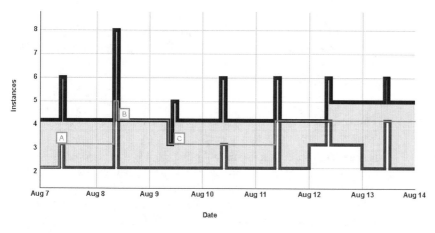

FIGURE 3
Using constraint rules with maximum and minimum values without reactive rules

This scenario uses a number of different constraint rules with different maximum and minimum values. You can see how the instance count always remains between the minimum and maximum limits.

The reconciliation algorithm that the Autoscaling Application Block uses when it evaluates constraint rules works as follows:

- If the current instance count is less than the minimum instance count specified by the constraint rules at the current time, then increase the current instance count to the minimum value. This occurs at label A on the diagram.

- If the current instance count is greater than the maximum instance count specified by the constraint rules at the current time, then decrease the current instance count to the maximum value. This occurs at label B on the diagram.

- Otherwise, leave the current instance count unchanged. This occurs at label C on the diagram.

Reactive Rules

It is not always possible to predict when demand will increase for your application or when there will be temporary bursts of demand. The Autoscaling Application Block also allows you to create reactive rules that trigger a scaling action when an aggregate value derived from a set of data points exceeds a certain threshold.

The Autoscaling Application Block can monitor the value of performance counters, Windows Azure queue lengths, instance counts, and any custom-defined business metrics to scale the application when those values exceed specified thresholds. The application block refers to these values as *operands*, where an operand defines three things:

- The counter or metric
- The aggregate function, such as average or maximum
- The time interval over which the application block calculates the aggregate function

For example, the Autoscaling Application Block can monitor the CPU usage of your web role instances. When the CPU usage performance counter average for the last hour goes above a threshold of 80%, the rule will perform an action to add new web role instances to handle this load, which should cause the average CPU usage levels to drop (assuming the load does not increase significantly). It will continue to add web role instances until the average CPU usage falls below the threshold. The reverse works as well. For example, if the average CPU usage over the last hour falls below a threshold of 40% then the rule will perform an action to remove web role instances until the average CPU usage is above the threshold value. Reactive rules can adjust the role instance account by an absolute number or by a proportion.

Typically, reactive rules are paired with one rule to scale up/out and another to scale down/in.

Reactive rules use an expression to specify a condition to evaluate to determine whether the rule should perform a scaling action. The actions that a reactive rule can trigger include:

- Changing the instance count value of the rule's target. The action can increment or decrement the count by a number or by a proportion.
- Changing the configuration of a hosted service. This action provides new values for entries in the application's ServiceConfiguration.cscfg file.
- Sending a notification to an operator.
- Switching to a different operating mode when you have configured your application to use application throttling.
- Executing a custom action.

  An action generates a notification if the action fails.

  If your application uses multiple web and worker roles, you will need to define an action for each web and worker role that you want to scale. You can use scale groups to simplify this task.

  Example reactive rules include:
- If the CPU utilization performance counter, averaged over the last hour for worker role A (across all instances) is greater than 80%, then perform an action.

- If the minimum length of a Windows Azure queue over the last six hours was greater than 50, then perform an action.

Rules can have a simple Boolean expression that compares a single value to a threshold, or a complex expression that includes a Boolean combination of multiple comparisons based on multiple operands. An example rule with a complex expression is:

- If CPU utilization averaged for the last hour was growing, and the queue length remained above 120 for the last two hours, then perform an action.

Figure 4 illustrates the behavior of the Autoscaling Application Block when you have a reactive rule defined in addition to multiple constraint rules. The scenario displayed in the diagram uses three separate constraint rules to determine the minimum and maximum number of instances of worker role A in your application.

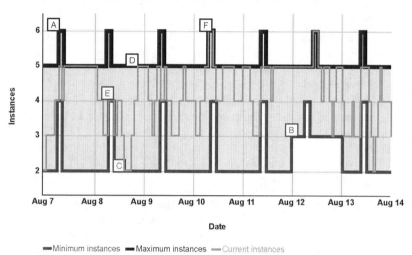

FIGURE 4
Constraint rules interacting with reactive rules

The three constraint rules that are in effect for worker role A are as follows:

1. The first constraint rule is always active. It sets the minimum number of instances for worker role A to two and the maximum to five. It has the lowest ranking.

2. The second constraint rule is active between 8:00 AM and 10:00 AM every day (Label A on the diagram shows when this rule becomes active for the first time). It sets the minimum number of instances for worker role A to four and the maximum to six. It has the highest ranking of the three rules, so when it overlaps with any other rules it takes precedence.

3. The third constraint rule is active every Friday (in the diagram, 12 August is a Friday, Label B on the diagram shows when this rule becomes active). It sets the minimum number of instances for worker role A to three and the maximum to five. It has a lower ranking than the second rule, so between 8:00 AM and 10:00 AM on Fridays, the second rule overrides this rule.

In addition, there are two reactive rules that can adjust the instance count of worker role A:

- If the minimum number of unprocessed documents during the last hour was greater than 10, then increase the instance count of worker role A by one.

- If the maximum number of unprocessed documents during the last hour was less than 10, then decrease the instance count of worker role A by one.

In the scenario shown in Figure 4, you can see how the constraint rules always limit the number of instances, providing absolute floor and ceiling values that cannot be crossed. The reactive rules can adjust the number of role instances within these limits. In the diagram, labels C and D show times when the first constraint rule enforced limits on the number of instances that the reactive rule proposed. Labels E and F show times when the second constraint rule enforced limits on the number of instances that the reactive rule proposed; at these times, the second constraint rule overrides the first constraint rule.

> *If there is no constraint rule active for a role when the rule evaluation process runs, and a reactive rule tries to change the number of role instances, then the Autoscaling Application Block will log a message that it cannot perform any scaling actions on the role. The block will not change the current number of role instances.*

A rule can perform one or more actions.

You should be careful about assigning ranks to your reactive rules. It is better to rely on the reconciliation process to determine which scaling action should be performed.

Multiple reactive rules can trigger different, conflicting actions at the same time. In this case, the Autoscaling Application Block can reconcile the conflicting actions.

For more information about how the block reconciles conflicting rules, see the topic *"Understanding Rule Ranks and Reconciliation"* on MSDN.

Logging

Whether you use instance autoscaling, application throttling, or a combination of the two approaches, the Autoscaling Application Block can log information about its activities. For example, it can write a log entry:

- When it starts or stops new instances, and include information about why the Autoscaling Application Block added this instance.
- When the application switches between various modes of operation, and include information about what triggered the throttling behavior.

You can use this information to help analyze your Windows Azure costs, and to identify predictable patterns in the utilization levels of your application.

THE AUTOSCALING LIFECYCLE

Figure 5 illustrates the lifecycle of the autoscaling process from the perspective of operations personnel.

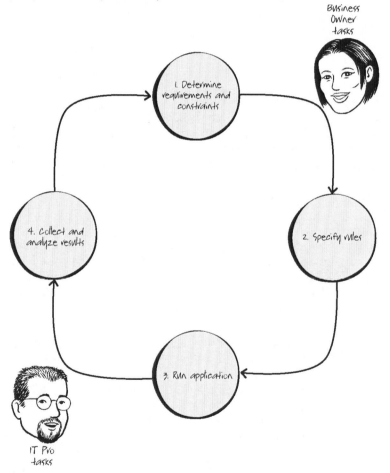

FIGURE 5
The lifecycle of the autoscaling process

The lifecycle of the autoscaling process consists of four stages that operations staff can iterate over multiple times as they refine the autoscaling behavior of your application.

Determine Requirements and Constraints

The first stage is to determine the requirements and constraints for autoscaling behavior in your application. To determine the two types of requirements, you must:

- Identify any predictable patterns of demand for your application's services.
- Specify how you want your application to respond to unpredicted bursts and collapses in demand for its services.

    The possible constraints you will face include:
- Budgetary constraints on the running costs of your Windows Azure application.
- Any commitments to an SLA with your application's users.

Specify Rules

Based on the requirements and constraints that you identified in the previous step, you must formulate a set of rules to specify the autoscaling behavior of the application within your constraints. You can use constraint rules to define the behavior of the application in response to predictable changes in demand, and reactive rules to define the behavior of the application in response to unpredictable changes in demand.

Run the Application

After you have configured the rules, the Autoscaling Application Block can evaluate the rules and execute the autoscaling actions in your application as the application faces real changes in demand. The Autoscaling Application Block will log the rule evaluation results and the autoscaling actions that it performs.

Collect and Analyze the Results

You should regularly analyze the information that the Autoscaling Application Block logs about its activities in order to evaluate how well your rules are meeting your initial requirements and working within the constraints. For example, you may discover that your rules do not always enable your application to scale sufficiently to meet demand or that the rules are preventing you from meeting your SLA commitments in all circumstances. In these cases, you should re-evaluate your requirements and constraints to ensure that they are still valid and, if necessary, adjust your rules. You may be able to identify new, predictable usage patterns that will allow you to preemptively scale your application rather than relying on reactive rules.

You should continue to iterate over this process because usage patterns for your application will change over time and the existing set of rules may become sub-optimal for your requirements and constraints.

When Should You Use the Autoscaling Application Block?

This section describes three scenarios in which you should consider using the Autoscaling Application Block in your Windows Azure solution.

YOU WANT YOUR APPLICATION TO RESPOND AUTOMATICALLY TO CHANGES IN DEMAND

The Autoscaling Application Block helps you to manage two competing requirements in your Windows Azure applications. The first is to maintain the performance levels of your application in the face of changing levels of demand. If your application's web or worker roles experience changes in their workload over time, varying significantly by the hour, the day, or the week, and you want your application to respond to these changes in demand automatically, then the Autoscaling Application Block can increase or decrease the number of role instances automatically based on pre-configured rules.

To keep users using your application, it must always be responsive.

New role instances can take at least 10 minutes to start up, so you can also use the application throttling feature of the Autoscaling Application Block when you need to respond quickly (within seconds or minutes) to a burst in activity.

YOU WANT TO MANAGE THE COSTS ASSOCIATED WITH RUNNING YOUR APPLICATION

The second, competing requirement is to minimize the running costs of your Windows Azure application. Although additional web and worker role instances will enable your application to maintain response times for users and maintain throughput for background tasks when there is a burst in activity, these additional role instances cost money. Windows Azure bills for web and worker role instances by the hour, and these compute costs are typically a large proportion of the running costs of a Windows Azure application. For a more detailed discussion of how you can estimate your Windows Azure running costs, see the chapter *"How Much Will It Cost?"* in the book *"Moving Applications to the Cloud."*

The profitability of the application is directly affected by its running costs.

The Autoscaling Application Block helps to manage costs by removing unnecessary role instances and by allowing you to set maximum values for the number of role instances. However, there may be circumstances in which your application sees an additional burst in activity when it is already running the maximum configured number

of instances. In this case, your application can respond by using application throttling. The throttling rules can define when your application should switch to an operating mode that is less resource intensive or disable non-critical functionality. In this way, the application can maintain the responsiveness of its UI or the throughput of critical processes without starting additional role instances.

YOU HAVE PREDICTABLE TIMES WHEN YOUR APPLICATION REQUIRES ADDITIONAL RESOURCES

The rules used by the Autoscaling Application Block allow you to define when the number of role instances should increase or decrease. When you know in advance that there will be a burst in demand, you can start additional role instances before the burst takes place by using autoscaling rules to define a timetable that specifies the number of roles that should be available at particular times.

WHEN SHOULD YOU NOT USE THE AUTOSCALING APPLICATION BLOCK

There are some scenarios in which you should not use the Autoscaling Application Block in your Windows Azure application.

Simple Applications

Autoscaling does not often add much value for relatively simple applications or applications that have a limited number of users. For example, many small web applications never need more than two web role instances, even during bursts of activity.

Adding the Autoscaling Application Block to your application increases the complexity of your application. Therefore, you should evaluate whether or not the benefits of adding autoscaling behavior outweigh the additional complexity to the design of your application.

> You can collect and analyze historic data and use your knowledge of external factors that trigger changes in demand to help predict workloads.

> You should consider designing your application to be scalable, even if your application does not require scalability right now. Usually, you cannot make an existing application scalable without having to re-engineer it.

Controlling Costs

If you want to treat some of the costs of your Windows Azure application as fixed costs, then you may want to fix the number of role instances in your application. This way, you can predict the exact cost of this portion of your monthly Windows Azure bill. You cannot treat all Windows Azure costs as fixed costs: for example, data transfer costs and Windows Azure storage costs will always vary based on the quantity of data you are transferring and storing.

Applications That Are Not Scalable

Autoscaling only makes sense for applications that you design to be scalable. If your application is not horizontally scalable, because its design is such that you cannot improve its performance by adding additional instances, then you should not use the Autoscaling Application Block to perform instance autoscaling. For example, a simple web role may not be scalable because it uses a session implementation that is not web farm friendly. For a discussion of session state in Windows Azure applications, see *Storing Session State* in the book "*Moving Applications to the Cloud, 2nd Edition.*" For a discussion of some of the design issues associated with scalable worker roles, see *Scaling Applications by Using Worker Roles* in the book "*Developing Applications for the Cloud, 2nd Edition.*"

Using the Autoscaling Application Block

Using the Autoscaling Application Block includes tasks that developers perform and tasks that IT pros perform. Figure 6 relates the key tasks to the actions of the Autoscaling Application Block in Windows Azure.

The Autoscaling Application Block automates the scaling process for applications that are already scalable. Using the Autoscaling Application Block does not automatically make your application scalable.

FIGURE 6
Using the
Autoscaling
Application
Block

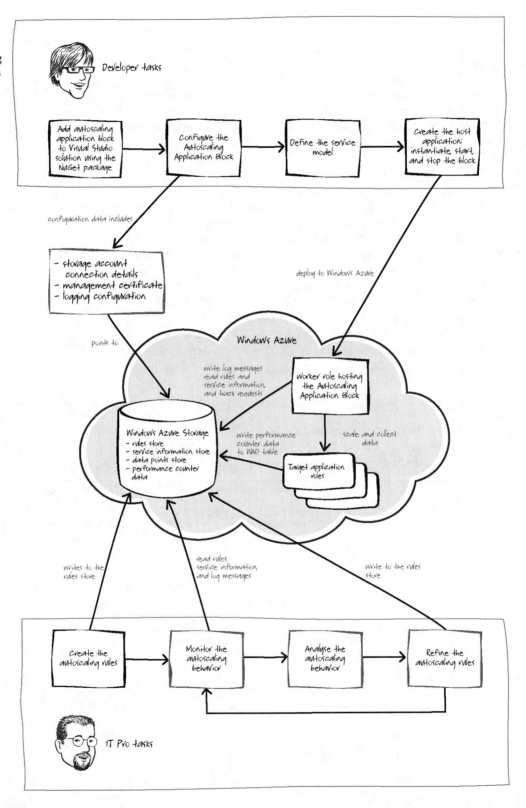

This section describes, at a high level, how to use the Autoscaling Application Block. It is divided into the following main sub-sections. The order of these sections reflects the order in which you would typically perform the associated tasks. Developers will perform some of these tasks and administrators will perform others. The description of each task suggests who, in practice, is likely to perform each one.

- **Adding the Autoscaling Application Block to your Visual Studio Project**. This section describes how you, as a developer, can prepare your Microsoft Visual Studio® development system solution to use the block.

- **Hosting the autoscaling application block**. This section describes how you, as a developer, can host the Autoscaling Application Block in your Windows Azure application.

- **Changes to your Windows Azure application**. This section describes the changes that you need to make in your Windows Azure application so that it works with the Autoscaling Application Block.

- **The service information**. This section describes how you, as a developer, define your application's service information.

- **Adding throttling behavior to your application**. This section describes how you, as a developer, can modify your application so that it can be throttled by your autoscaling rules.

- **The autoscaling rules**. This section describes how you, as an administrator, can define your autoscaling rules.

- **Monitoring the Autoscaling Application Block**. This section describes how you, as an administrator, can monitor your autoscaling rules and how to use the data that you collect.

- **Advanced usage scenarios**. This section describes some additional scenarios, such as using scale groups and extending the Autoscaling Application Block.

ADDING THE AUTOSCALING APPLICATION BLOCK TO YOUR VISUAL STUDIO PROJECT

As a developer, before you can write any code that uses the Autoscaling Application Block, you must configure your Visual Studio project with all of the necessary assemblies, references, and other resources that you'll need. For information about how you can use NuGet to prepare your Visual Studio project to work with the Autoscaling Application Block, see the topic *"Adding the Autoscaling Application Block to a Host"* on MSDN.

You would typically perform this task when you are creating the host application for the block and work with the IT Pro to determine the required functionality.

NuGet makes it very easy for you to configure your project with all of the prerequisites for using the Autoscaling Application Block.

You can also download the NuGet package, extract the DLLs and add them to your project manually, or download the source code for the block and build it yourself.

You must decide where you will host the block: either in Windows Azure or in an on-premises application.

The Autoscaling Application Block is designed to work with very large Windows Azure applications with hundreds of different roles.

Hosting the Autoscaling Application Block

You can host the Autoscaling Application Block in a Windows Azure role or in an on-premises application such as a simple console application or a Windows service. This section discusses some of the reasons that you might choose one or the other of these approaches and provides links to resources that explain how to write the code that hosts the Autoscaling Application Block.

The Autoscaling Application Block enables you to add autoscaling behavior to your Windows Azure applications, and as such, it must be able to communicate with Windows Azure to make changes to the number of role instances that make up your application. Your Windows Azure application might be a simple application made up of a small number of roles, all running in the same hosted service in the same data center, or have hundreds of different roles running in multiple hosted services in multiple data centers. Whatever the structure of your application and wherever you choose to host the Autoscaling Application Block, it must be able to interact with your application by using the Windows Azure Service Management API, and it must be able to access diagnostic data such as performance counter values in order to evaluate reactive rules.

If you host the Autoscaling Application Block in Windows Azure, then you do not need to transfer any of the data that the application block uses out of the cloud. However, you may need to transfer diagnostic data between data centers if you host parts of your application in other geographical locations. The advantages of hosting the Autoscaling Application Block in Windows Azure are the same as for hosting any application in the cloud: reliability and scalability. However, you will need to pay to host the role that contains the application block in Windows Azure. You could host the application block in a worker role that also performs other tasks, but from the perspective of manageability and security you should host the application block in its own worker role or even in its own hosted service. For information about how to host the Autoscaling Application Block in Windows Azure, see the topic *"Hosting the Autoscaling Application Block in a Worker Role"* on MSDN.

Using the Autoscaling Application Block in code is very similar to using the other Enterprise Library application blocks. The topic *"Using Enterprise Library in Applications"* in the main Enterprise Library documentation describes how to reference the Enterprise Library assemblies, how Enterprise Library handles dependencies, and how to work with Enterprise Library objects.

If you choose to host the application block in Windows Azure, and plan to scale the role instance that hosts it for added reliability, you must make sure that you configure the application block to use a blob execution lease in the advanced configuration settings. This setting ensures that only a single instance of the application block is able to evaluate rules at any point in time. For information about how to make this configuration setting, see the topic *"Entering Configuration Information"* on MSDN.

> *The default configuration settings assume that you will have a single instance of the worker role that hosts the application block. You must change this if you plan to scale the role that hosts the Autoscaling Application Block.*

Hosting the application block on-premises means that the block must remotely access the diagnostic data from your Windows Azure application that it needs for reactive rules. An advantage of hosting the application block locally is that it may simplify integration with other tools and processes that run on premises. It may also be convenient to have the Autoscaling Application Block running locally when you are developing and testing your Windows Azure application. For information about how to host the Autoscaling Application Block in an on-premises application, see the topic *"Hosting the Autoscaling Application Block in an On-Premises Application"* on MSDN.

CHANGES TO YOUR WINDOWS AZURE APPLICATION

The Autoscaling Application Block is designed to minimize the changes you need to make to your Windows Azure application. The application block can add and remove role instances from your application by using the Windows Azure Service Management API. This does not require any changes in your application.

However, reactive rules can use performance counter data to determine whether the application block should change the current number of role instances. If you are using performance counters in your reactive rules, then you must take steps to ensure that your application saves the performance counter data to Windows Azure storage where the application block's data collection process can access it.

For more information about the code changes you must make in your Windows Azure application to enable it to save performance counter data, see the topic *"Collecting Performance Counter Data"* on MSDN.

You can also use the Windows Azure Diagnostics Configuration File (diagnostics.wadcfg) to configure your performance counters. For more details, see *"How to Use the Windows Azure Diagnostics Configuration File"* on MSDN.

You can also instrument your Windows Azure application with custom performance counters to use in your reactive rules.

The service information defines the aspects of your Windows Azure application that are relevant to the Autoscaling Application Block.

THE SERVICE INFORMATION

Before the Autoscaling Application Block can perform any auto-scaling operations on your Windows Azure application, you need to configure the service information that describes your Windows Azure application. By default, this service information is stored in an XML document in a Windows Azure blob that is accessible to the application block.

The service information includes the following information about the Windows Azure features that make up your application.

• For each Windows Azure subscription that contains resources that you want to be able to scale automatically, the service information contains the subscription ID, certificate thumbprint, and details of where the application block can find the management certificate it needs to be able to issue scaling requests.

• For each Windows Azure hosted service that contains resources that you want to be able to scale automatically, the service information contains the names of the deployment slots where the application to be scaled is running.

• The application block can only use the Windows Azure roles that are listed in the service information as sources of performance counter data or as targets for autoscaling. For each role listed in the service information, the service information identifies the storage account where Windows Azure saves the role's diagnostic data. The application block reads the performance counter data that the reactive rules use from this storage account.

• The names of any queues whose length the application block monitors.

• The definitions of the scale groups. These are described later in this chapter.

The Autoscaling Application Block rules can only operate on targets (roles and scale groups) that are identified in the application block's service information. For further information see the topic *"Storing Your Service Information Data"* on MSDN.

The service information also enables you to control how aggressively you want to autoscale your Windows Azure application by specifying cool-down periods. A *cool-down period* is the period after a scaling operation has taken place during which the application block will not perform any further scaling operations. A cool-down period is enabled via the optimizing stabilizer feature of the application block. You can define different cool-down periods for scale-up and scale-down operations, and specify default cool-down periods that individual roles can override. The shorter the cool-down period, the more aggressive the application block will be in issuing scaling requests. However, by setting short cool-down periods for both scale-up and scale-down operations, you risk introducing an oscillation whereby the application block repeatedly scales up and then scales down a role. If not specified, the application block uses a default of 20 minutes for the cool-down period.

The service information also enables you to configure when, during the hour, you want to allow scaling operations to take place. Because Windows Azure bills by the clock hour, you may want to use role instances for as long as possible within an hour. To achieve this, you can specify that scale up operations can only take place during the first X minutes of the hour and that scale down operations can only take place during the last Y minutes of the hour.

There is no point in setting cool-down periods to less than ten minutes. Windows Azure can often take ten minutes to complete a scaling operation on a role, during which time it will not accept any additional scaling requests for that role anyway.

> *You need to allow enough time for the scale down operations to complete before the end of the hour. Otherwise, you will be billed for the next hour.*

With the exception of scale groups, which are a convenience when it comes to authoring rules, the developers of the application typically define the service information; they know about the structure of the application, and what can and cannot be safely scaled.

Using the Autoscaling Application Block does not automatically make your Windows Azure roles scalable. Although Windows Azure provides the infrastructure that enables your applications to scale, you are responsible for ensuring that your web and worker roles will run correctly when there is more than one instance of the role. For example, it may not be possible to parallelize some algorithms.

> *See the section "The Map Reduce Algorithm" in the book Developing Applications for the Cloud for information about a technique for parallelizing large calculations across multiple role instances.*

You should ensure that your service information data only references roles that are scalable.

For web roles to be scalable, they should be "web farm friendly." In particular, if they make use of session state, then the session state provider either shares or synchronizes your session state data across your role instances. In Windows Azure, you can use the session state provider that stores session state in the shared cache. For more information, see "*Session State Provider*" on MSDN.

> *To minimize the risk of disclosing sensitive information, you should encrypt the contents of the service information store. For more information, see the topic "Encrypting the Rules Store and the Service Information Store" on MSDN.*

ADDING THROTTLING BEHAVIOR TO YOUR APPLICATION

The Autoscaling Application Block enables you to use two different autoscaling mechanisms in your Windows Azure applications. You can either use autoscaling rules to change the number of role instances or use autoscaling rules to modify the behavior of your application, typically by *throttling* the application so that it uses fewer resources. Examples of throttling behavior include temporarily disabling some non-essential features in your application, and switching to a less resource-intensive version of the UI.

There are two scenarios in which you might decide to use throttling.

- You can use throttling instead of instance autoscaling for some or all of the roles in your application. You might chose to do this if your role does not support running with multiple instances or because you can achieve better scaling results by changing the behavior of the role rather than adding or removing new instances.

- You want your application to respond almost immediately to a burst in demand. With throttling, you can change the behavior of the application as soon as the application block executes a reactive rule action without having to wait for Windows Azure to start a new role instance. Depending on the size and complexity of your application, throttling may not take effect faster than instance scaling.

To add throttling behavior to your Windows Azure application you must modify your application to respond to requests for it. For more information about how your Windows Azure application can detect a request for throttling behavior, see the topic *"Implementing Throttling Behavior"* on MSDN.

You must also create a set of reactive rules that use the **change-Setting** action to notify your application that it should enable or disable some throttling behavior. For information about how to define the throttling autoscaling rules, see the topic *"Defining Throttling Autoscaling Rules"* on MSDN.

For a complete example of how the Tailspin Surveys application uses throttling behavior, see Chapter 5, *"Making Tailspin Surveys More Elastic"* in this guide.

Using Instance Autoscaling and Throttling Together

You can use instance autoscaling exclusively or throttling exclusively in your Windows Azure application, or use them together.

If you decide to use them together, you need to take into account how they will interact. You should be aware of a number of differences between them when you are creating your autoscaling rules.

- Instance autoscaling rules can take up to ten minutes to have an effect because of the time taken by Windows Azure to launch new role instances. Throttling autoscaling rules can affect the behavior of your application almost immediately.

- Instance autoscaling rules are limited by the configurable cool-down periods that set a minimum time before the application block can scale the same role again; there are no cool-down periods for throttling autoscaling rules.

- Instance autoscaling rules are always limited by constraint rules. Throttling autoscaling rules are not limited by constraint rules.

A single reactive rule can have an action that performs instance autoscaling and an action that performs throttling.

You can use rule ranks to control the precedence of reactive rules that perform instance autoscaling and reactive rules that perform throttling.

THE AUTOSCALING RULES

Autoscaling actions take place in response to rules that define when the Autoscaling Application Block should scale roles up or down. By default, these rules are stored in an XML document in a Windows Azure blob that is accessible to the application block.

The next chapter describes a Windows Azure application with an example of a web-based UI for managing rules.

The Autoscaling Application Block supports two types of rules that define autoscaling behavior: *constraint rules* and *reactive rules*. Typically, the administrators of the application are responsible for creating, monitoring, and maintaining these rules. They can perform these tasks by editing the XML document that contains the rules, or through a user interface (UI) created by the developers of the application.

When you are creating your autoscaling rules, you can only create rules for the roles that the developers listed in the service information. You should plan your rules in three stages:

1. Design the default (or "baseline") constraint rules.

2. Design any additional constraint rules.

3. Design your reactive rules.

You should create a default constraint rule for every role that is listed in the service information. A default rule does not have a time-table, so it is always active; it has a rank of zero, so it can be overridden by any other constraint rules; it should have minimum and maximum role instance values that define the default values you want when no other constraint rules are active. These default rules should ensure that you always have the minimum number of role instances that you need to meet your SLA commitments, and that you don't go over budget by running too many role instances.

Default rules guard your SLAs!

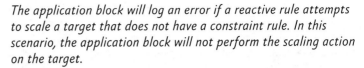

The application block will log an error if a reactive rule attempts to scale a target that does not have a constraint rule. In this scenario, the application block will not perform the scaling action on the target.

After you have created your default rules, you can define any additional constraint rules that handle expected periods of above or below normal workload for your application. These additional constraint rules have timetables that specify when the rule is active, a rank that is greater than one to ensure that they override the default constraint rules, and appropriate values for the maximum and minimum role instance counts. For example, your application might experience increased workloads at 9:00 AM to 10:00 AM every morning, or on the last Friday of every month, or decreased workloads between 1:00 PM and 5:00 PM every day, or during the month of August.

If you want to specify a fixed number of instances for a role, you can use a constraint rule with the maximum and minimum values set to the same number. In this case, reactive rules will not have any effect on the number of role instances.

The constraint rules enable you to plan for expected changes in workload.

The reactive rules enable you to plan for unexpected changes in your application's workload. A reactive rule works by monitoring an aggregate value derived from a set of data points such as performance counter values, and then performing a scaling operation when the aggregate value reaches a threshold. The challenge with reactive rules is knowing which aggregates and data points, or combination of aggregates and data points, you should use in your reactive rules. For

Default rules guard your wallet!

You may already have a good idea about when your application's workload changes based on your knowledge and experience of the application and your organization. However, you will gain a deeper insight by monitoring and analyzing your application.

You must monitor and analyze the behavior of your application to understand what data points and aggregates, or combination of data points and aggregates, work best as a proxy measure of your application's performance. You may need multiple rules because different aspects of your application may have different performance characteristics.

example, if you have a reactive rule that monitors CPU utilization, but your application is I/O bound, the reactive rule won't trigger a scaling action at the correct time. Another example is if you have a reactive rule that monitors the length of a Windows Azure queue. If it doesn't matter to the functionality of the application if the queue is emptied later, you will be wasting resources if you scale up to clear the queue earlier than is necessary.

If performance counters or Windows Azure queue lengths don't work well as ways of measuring your application's performance, the application's developers can instrument the application to generate custom business metrics to use in rules.

If your reactive rules use performance counter data from your Windows Azure application, you must make sure that your application transfers the performance counter data that the rules consume to Windows Azure Diagnostics storage. For an example of how to do this, see the section "Collecting Performance Counter Data from Tailspin Surveys" in Chapter 5, *"Making Tailspin Surveys More Elastic"* of this guide.

For information about defining rules, see the section "Rules and Actions" earlier in this chapter.

> *To minimize the risk of disclosing sensitive information, you should encrypt the contents of the rules store. For more information, see the topic* "Encrypting the Rules Store and the Service Information Store" *on MSDN.*

Implementing Schedule-based Autoscaling Without Reactive Rules

In some scenarios, you may want to use a schedule to precisely control the number of role instances at different times. You may want to do this because you want your running costs to be more predictable, or because you do not anticipate any unexpected bursts in demand for your application. You can achieve this goal by using only constraint rules and not reactive rules. Furthermore, your constraint rules should each have the maximum instance count equal to the minimum instance count.

The following snippet shows a simple set of rules that implement schedule-based autoscaling without using reactive rules. The default constraint rule sets the role instance count to two, the peak-time rule sets the role instance count to four.

```XML
<rules
  xmlns=http://schemas.microsoft.com/practices/2011/entlib/
autoscaling/rules
  enabled="true">
  <constraintRules>
    <rule name="Default" description="Always active"
         enabled="true" rank="1">
      <actions>
        <range min="2" max="2" target="RoleA"/>
      </actions>
    </rule>

    <rule name="Peak" description="Active at peak times"
         enabled="true" rank="100">
      <actions>
        <range min="4" max="4" target="RoleA"/>
      </actions>
      <timetable startTime="08:00:00" duration="02:00:00">
        <daily/>
      </timetable>
    </rule>
  </constraintRules>

  <reactiveRules/>

  <operands/>
</rules>
```

MONITORING THE AUTOSCALING APPLICATION BLOCK

Over time, usage patterns for your application will change. The overall number of users will go up or down, people will start to use the application at different times, the application may gain new features, and people will use some parts of the application less and some parts more. As a consequence, your constraint and reactive rules may no longer deliver the optimal balance of performance and cost.

The Autoscaling Application Block logs detailed information about the behavior of your rules so you can analyze which rules were triggered and at what times. This information, in combination with other performance monitoring data that you collect, will help you analyze the effectiveness of your rule set and determine what changes you should make to re-optimize the rules.

The Autoscaling Application Block can use the Enterprise Library Logging Block logger, System. Diagnostics logging, or a custom logger.

How frequently you analyze your rule behavior depends on how dynamic the environment is within which your application operates.

For information about the logging data that the application block generates, see the topic *"Autoscaling Application Block Logging"* on MSDN.

Figure 7 shows the data sources you may want to use when you are analyzing the behavior of the Autoscaling Application Block and your application.

> Keeping your autoscaling rules optimized for your specific requirements is an ongoing task that you must plan for.

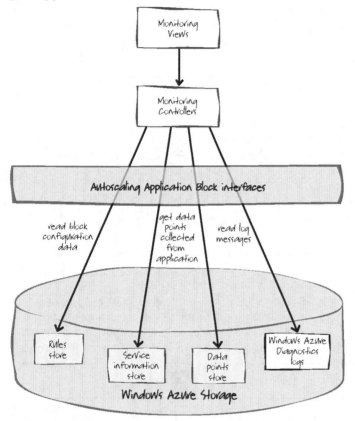

FIGURE 7
Monitoring your autoscaling behavior

The application block provides interfaces that enable you to read its configuration information, the autoscaling rules, and the service information from the stores. You can also access the data points collected by the application block, such as performance counters and queue lengths that it uses when it evaluates the reactive rules. The application block also provides some methods that help you read and parse log messages that it has generated and written to the Windows Azure Diagnostics log table using the system diagnostics logging infrastructure.

For more information about reading from the rules store, see the **IRulesStore** *interface* in the API documentation.

For more information about reading from the service information store, see the **IServiceInformationStore** *Interface* in the API documentation.

For more information about reading from the rules store, see the **IDataPointsStore** *Interface* in the API documentation.

For more information about reading and parsing the Autoscaling Application Block log messages, see the topic *"Reading the Autoscaling Application Block Log Messages."*

For a complete example of using the different data sources to visualize the Autoscaling Application Block activities, see the section "Visualizing the Autoscaling Actions" in Chapter 5, *"Making Tailspin Surveys More Elastic."*

ADVANCED USAGE SCENARIOS

This section provides guidance about when you should use some of the advanced features of the Autoscaling Application Block.

Scale Groups

In an application with many web and worker roles, you may find it difficult to create and manage the large number of rules you need to define the autoscaling behavior in your application. In this scenario, scale groups provide a convenient way to define rules that can act on multiple roles at once. You should define the scale groups you need before you start creating rules.

To define a scale group, you must identify the roles that will make up the scale group, and assign each role type in the scale group a ratio. The block uses these ratios to calculate the number of instances of each member of the scale group when it performs a scaling action. The following table shows a small example scale group; in practice, scale groups are likely to consist of many more targets.

Scale groups are a convenience. They help to minimize the number of rules you need to create and manage.

Target	Ratio
Target A (Worker role A in Service Host A)	2
Target B (Worker role A in Service Host B)	1
Target C (Web role A in Service Host A)	3

A scale group can include targets that refer to roles in different hosted services.

The application block does not use transactions to perform operations on the members of a scale group and scale groups do not guarantee to preserve the ratios between the role instances. For example, a constraint rule may limit the number of instances suggested by a reactive rule for some roles in a scale group, or an operator may manually change the number of instances of one or more roles independently of your autoscaling rules.

A reactive rule can use a scale group as its target. The following table shows the effect of scaling the scale group by an increment of two using the ratios shown in the previous table.

Target	Initial instance count	Instance count after scaling
Target A	4	8
Target B	2	4
Target C	6	12

The result is calculated as follows:

(Initial instance count) + (Increment * Ratio)

The following table shows the effect of a reactive rule scaling the scale group by 50%.

Target	Initial instance count	Instance count after scaling
Target A	4	8
Target B	2	3
Target C	6	15

The result is calculated as follows:

(Initial instance count)
+
(Increment * Ratio * Initial instance count)

You can also use scale groups when you specify constraint rules. A constraint rule uses the ratios to determine the maximum and minimum values of the role instance counts. An example constraint rule specifies a maximum count of five and a minimum count of two. The following table shows the maximum and minimum instance count values of the individual roles that make up our example scale group.

Target	Minimum instance count	Maximum instance count
Target A	4	10
Target B	2	5
Target C	6	15

Using Different Ratios at Different Times

You can use multiple scale groups with the same members to apply different ratios at different times. For example, you could define the two scale groups shown in the following tables:

Scale Group A

Target	Ratio
Target A (Worker role A in Service Host A)	2
Target B (Worker role A in Service Host B)	1
Target C (Web role A in Service Host A)	3

Scale Group B

Target	Ratio
Target A (Worker role A in Service Host A)	3
Target B (Worker role A in Service Host B)	1
Target C (Web role A in Service Host A)	1

You could then define two rules, as shown in the following table:

Rule name	Timetable	Rank	Target
Default rule	Always active	1	Scale Group A
Batch processing rule	Sundays between 2:00 and 4:00	20	Scale Group B

> Don't make things too complicated by putting a role into too many scale groups. It will make it more difficult for you to understand why the Autoscaling Application Block has set a particular instance count value.

Both rules target the same roles, but apply different ratios. The batch processing constraint rule will override the default constraint rule on Sundays between 2:00 and 4:00 in the morning and use the ratios defined for scale group B.

Using Notifications

You may decide that you want to preview any scaling operations suggested by the Autoscaling Application Block before the application block sends them to Windows Azure. This may be useful when you are testing the block and want to double check the scaling operations before they happen, or if you want to use the operator's knowledge of the application to refine your autoscaling rules and "tweak" the scaling actions.

> *The application block can send notifications and performs scaling actions at the same time so that operators are notified of the scaling operations that the application block performs.*

You can configure the application block to send an email message to one or more operators/administrators. The email message provides full details of all of the scaling operations that the application block suggested based on the current set of autoscaling rules.

For more information about how to configure notifications, see the topic *"Using Notifications and Manual Scaling"* on MSDN.

> You can use notifications while you are evaluating or testing the block. The notifications can tell you what operations the block would perform given the current set of rules.

Integrating with the Application Lifecycle

When you deploy an application to Windows Azure, you can deploy to either the staging or the production deployment slot. Typically, you deploy to the staging environment first, where you can perform any final tests before promoting the contents of the staging deployment to the production environment.

If you are testing your autoscaling behavior, you will need to have separate service information definitions and rules for each slot or modify the service information definition when you promote from staging to production.

The following code snippet from a service information definition file shows how the roles and scale groups are defined for the different deployment slots.

```xml
<?xml version="1.0" encoding="utf-8"?>
<serviceModel ... >
  <subscriptions>
    <subscription name="Autoscaling Sample" ...>
      <services>
        <service dnsPrefix="stagingautoscalingservice" slot="Staging">
          <roles>
            <role alias="Staging.AutoScaling.WebApp"
                  roleName="AutoScaling.WebApp" ... />
          </roles>
        </service>
        <service dnsPrefix="productionautoscalingservice" slot="Production">
          <roles>
            <role alias="Production.AutoScaling.WebApp"
                  roleName="AutoScaling.WebApp" ... />
          </roles>
        </service>
        <service dnsPrefix="stagingscalegroup" slot="Staging">
          <roles>
            <role alias="Staging.Autoscaling.Scalegroup.Billing"
                  roleName="Autoscaling.Scalegroup.Billing" ... />
            <role alias="Staging.Autoscaling.Scalegroup.BillProcessor"
                  roleName="Autoscaling.Scalegroup.BillProcessor" ... />
            <role alias="Staging.Autoscaling.Scalegroup.InvoiceReporting"
                  roleName="Autoscaling.Scalegroup.InvoiceReporting" ... />
          </roles>
        </service>
        <service dnsPrefix="productionscalegroup" slot="Production">
          <roles>
```

```
                <role alias="Production.Autoscaling.Scalegroup.Billing"
                      roleName="Autoscaling.Scalegroup.Billing" ... />
                <role alias="Production.Autoscaling.Scalegroup.BillProcessor"
                      roleName="Autoscaling.Scalegroup.BillProcessor" ... />
                <role alias="Production.Autoscaling.Scalegroup.InvoiceReporting"
                      roleName="Autoscaling.Scalegroup.InvoiceReporting" ... />
            </roles>
        </service>
      </services>
      <storageAccounts>
        ...
      </storageAccounts>
    </subscription>
  </subscriptions>

  <scaleGroups>
    <scaleGroup name="StagingScaleGroupA">
      <roles>
        <role roleAlias="Staging.Autoscaling.Scalegroup.Billing" ... />
        <role roleAlias="Staging.Autoscaling.Scalegroup.BillProcessor" ... />
        <role roleAlias="Staging.Autoscaling.Scalegroup.InvoiceReporting" ... />
      </roles>
    </scaleGroup>
    <scaleGroup name="ProductionScaleGroupA">
      <roles>
        <role roleAlias="Production.Autoscaling.Scalegroup.Billing" ... />
        <role roleAlias="Production.Autoscaling.Scalegroup.BillProcessor" ... />
        <role roleAlias="Production.Autoscaling.Scalegroup.InvoiceReporting" .../>
      </roles>
    </scaleGroup>
  </scaleGroups>
</serviceModel>
```

All role aliases and scale group names must be unique within the service information.

Extending the Autoscaling Application Block

In Enterprise Library, pretty much everything is extensible. The Autoscaling Application Block is no exception. It offers five key extension points if you want to extend or modify its functionality.

For more information, see the topic *"Extending and Modifying the Autoscaling Application Block"* on MSDN.

For more information, see the *"Extensibility Hands-on Labs for Microsoft Enterprise Library 5.0."*

You can also download the source code and make any changes you want. The license permits this.

Custom Actions

If you need to add a new action to the existing scaling and throttling actions, you can create a custom action. There are three steps to creating a custom action.

1. Create code that implements the action.

2. Create code that can deserialize your custom action from the rules store. If you are using the built-in rules store, this will require deserialization from XML.

3. Configure the application block to use the custom action.

For more information about custom actions, see the topic *"Creating a Custom Action"* on MSDN.

For an example of a custom action, see Chapter 5, *"Making Tailspin Surveys More Elastic."*

Custom Operands

In a reactive rule, an operand defines an aggregate value calculated from data points that the application block collects. If you need to add a new operand to the existing performance counter and queue length operands, you can create a custom operand. There are three steps to creating a custom operand.

1. Create code that implements a custom data collector.

2. Create code that can deserialize your custom operand from the rules store. If you are using the built-in rules store, this will require deserialization from XML.

3. Configure the application block to use the custom operand.

For more information about custom operands, see the topic *"Creating a Custom Operand"* on MSDN.

For an example of a custom operand, see Chapter 5, *"Making Tailspin Surveys More Elastic."*

By using custom operands, you can use business metrics in your rule definitions.

Custom Stores

The Autoscaling Application Block uses two stores, one for rules, and one for service information. For each of these stores, the application block includes two implementations: storing the data as XML in a Windows Azure blob or storing the data as XML in a file on the local file system. The first is used when you host the application block in a Windows Azure role, the second for when you host it in an on-premises application.

If you need to be able to manipulate your rules or service information in a different tool, you could replace these implementations with stores that store the data in a different format and in a different location; for example, JSON in a local file or in a SQL Server database.

For more information about creating a custom rules store, see the topic *"Creating a Custom Rules Store"* on MSDN.

For more information about creating a custom service information store, see the topic *"Creating a Custom Service Information Store"* on MSDN.

Custom Logging

The Autoscaling Application Block can use the logger in the **System. Diagnostics** namespace or the Enterprise Library Logging Application Block to log details of the autoscaling activities it performs.

If you want to use a different logging infrastructure, you can implement a custom logger for the application block. This may be useful if you want to integrate with your existing logging infrastructure to keep all your logs in a single location.

For more information about creating a custom logger, see the topic *"Creating a Custom Logger"* on MSDN.

Using the WASABiCmdlets

You can use the WASABiCmdlets Windows PowerShell® Cmdlets to perform operations on the Autoscaling Application Block from a Windows PowerShell script. With the WASABiCmdlets, you can enable and disable rules and rule evaluation, modify rule ranks, adjust the behavior of the stabilizer, and more.

In combination with the Windows Azure PowerShell Cmdlets, and System Center Operations Manager (SCOM) or other manageability tools, you can implement a powerful custom autoscaling solution.

For more information about the WASABiCmdlets, see the topic *"Using the WASABiCmdlets Windows PowerShell Cmdlets"* on MSDN.

For more information about the Windows Azure PowerShell Cmdlets, see *"Windows Azure PowerShell Cmdlets"* on CodePlex.

For more information about SCOM, see *"System Center Operations Manager"* on TechNet.

SAMPLE CONFIGURATION SETTINGS

The Autoscaling Application Block has a large number of configuration settings that you can use to control how it performs autoscaling for your application. This section describes some sample configurations to illustrate how you can configure the application block to address specific requirements. These illustrations are only guidelines: you should analyze your own requirements and the behavior of your Windows Azure application to determine the optimal configuration settings for your application.

These sample configurations refer to the Autoscaling Application Block configuration settings and to the autoscaling rules.

For more information about configuring the Autoscaling Application block, see the topic *"Entering Configuration Information"* on MSDN.

For more information about writing autoscaling rules, see the topics *"Defining Constraint Rules"* and *"Defining Reactive Rules"* on MSDN.

Determining the optimum set of timing values for a solution is usually an iterative process. During those iterations, you should take the timing values shown in the following table into consideration. The table shows the default values for the key configuration settings.

Configuration item	Location	Default value
Instance count collection interval	Hardcoded	Two minutes
Performance counter collection interval	Hardcoded	Two minutes
Queue length collection interval	Hardcoded	Two minutes
Rule evaluation interval	Configuration file	4 minutes
Tracking interval	Configuration file	5 minutes
Rules store monitoring interval: specifies how often the block checks for changes to the rules	Configuration file	30 seconds
Service information store monitoring interval: specifies how often the block checks for changes to the service information	Configuration file	30 seconds
Periods specified by constraint rules	Rules store	None
Operand timespan used to calculate aggregate values	Rules store	None

Cool-down periods (scaling up and down) used by the stabilizer	Service information store	20 minutes
Periods at the start and end of the hour when scaling operations do not occur	Service information store	None
Windows Azure related timings such as WAD transfer rate and performance counter sampling rates.	Windows Azure configuration or application code	None

Figure 8 illustrates the relationships between some of the timing configuration settings in the previous table.

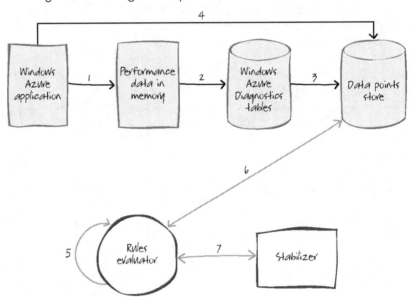

FIGURE 8
Timing relationships

The following list explains what is happening at each point on the diagram:

1. Your Windows Azure application captures performance monitoring data. You typically configure these counters either in the **OnStart** method of your Windows Azure roles, or through Windows Azure configuration. This data is captured in memory.

2. Your Windows Azure application saves the performance monitoring data to the Windows Azure diagnostics (WAD)

tables. You typically configure transfer periods either in the **OnStart** method of your Windows Azure roles, or through Windows Azure configuration.

3. The Autoscaling Application Block collects performance counter data from the Windows Azure diagnostics tables and saves it in the data points store. This happens every two minutes. This value is hardcoded in the application block.

4. The Autoscaling Application Block collects instance count, queue length, and any custom metrics data from your Windows Azure application and saves it in the data points store. This happens every two minutes. This value is hardcoded in the application block.

For Windows Azure infrastructure-related timings such as WAD transfer periods and performance counter sampling rates you need to determine timings for your application scenario. Don't assume that a one minute transfer period is best for all scenarios.

5. The rules evaluator runs and identifies the autoscaling rules that apply at the current point in time. The frequency at which the rules evaluator runs is specified in the configuration file. The default value is four minutes.

6. The rules evaluator retrieves the data points that it needs from the data points store. The amount of data for each rule is determined by the time span of the operand associated with the rule. For example, if the operand specifies an average over ten minutes, the rules evaluator retrieves data from the last ten minutes from the data points store.

7. The stabilizer may prevent certain scaling operations from happening. For example, the stabilizer may specify cool-down periods after the application block has performed a scaling operation or limit scaling operations to certain periods in the hour.

The following sections suggest some configuration settings for specific scenarios.

Average Rule Evaluation Period

You have a web application that gets busy at some times that are hard to predict. If you begin to see an increase in the number of rejected web requests over the past five minutes, you want to take action now, in order to ensure that within the next 20 minutes you will have enough resources available to handle the increase in the number of requests. You are willing to accept that some requests may continue to be rejected for the next 20 minutes.

You also have a predictable usage pattern, so you will also use constraint rules to ensure that you reserve enough instances at the times when you know there will be a higher number of requests.

Remember that Windows Azure takes time to start up new role instances, so in this scenario you must expect some requests to be rejected while this is happening.

The following table shows some sample configuration values for this scenario.

Configuration item	Default value
Rule evaluation interval	Five minutes
Tracking interval	Five minutes
Instance count collection interval	Two minutes (hardcoded)
Performance counter collection interval	Two minutes (hardcoded)
Queue length collection interval	Two minutes (hardcoded)
Cool-down period (both for scaling up and down)	20 minutes
Operand: ASP.NET application restarts	30 minutes
Operand: ASP.NET Requests queued	15 minutes
Operand: ASP.NET requests rejected	5 minutes

Long Rule Evaluation Period

Typically, your application has a very stable and constant level of demand, but it does occasionally encounter moderate increases in usage. Therefore, you decide to evaluate your autoscaling rules every 30 minutes and look for higher than average CPU utilization. You also have a scale-down rule that runs when CPU utilization starts to fall back to its normal level.

The following table shows some sample configuration values for this scenario.

Configuration item	Default value
Rule evaluation interval	30 minutes
Tracking interval	Five minutes
Instance count collection interval	Two minutes (hardcoded)
Performance counter collection interval	Two minutes (hardcoded)
Queue length collection interval	Two minutes (hardcoded)
Cool-down period (both for scaling up and down)	20 minutes
Operand: CPU Utilization %	30 minutes

Configuring the Stabilizer

The stabilizer performs two functions for the Autoscaling Application Block: it helps to prevent fast oscillations (the "yo-yo effect") in the number of role instances by defining cool-down periods, and it helps to optimize costs by limiting scaling-up operations to the beginning of the hour and scaling-down operations to the end of the hour.

The following snippet from a service information definition shows an example of the stabilizer configuration.

XML

```
<stabilizer scaleUpCooldown="00:20:00"
            scaleDownCooldown="00:30:00"
    scaleUpOnlyInFirstMinutesOfHour="15"
    scaleDownOnlyInLastMinutesOfHour="10"
    notificationsCooldown="00:25:00">
    <role roleAlias="BillingWorkerRole"
        scaleUpCooldown="00:18:00"
        scaleDownCooldown="00:18:00" />
</stabilizer>
```

> *You can configure global stabilizer settings and override them for specific roles.*

In this example, the **scaleUpCooldown** setting prevents the application block from scaling up a role for 20 minutes after any change in the instance count for that role. Similarly, the **scaleDownCooldown** setting prevents the application block from scaling down a role for 30 minutes after any change in the instance count for that role.

The **scaleUpOnlyInFirstMinutesOfHour** setting ensures that the application block only performs scale up operations during the first 15 minutes of the hour, and the **scaleDownOnlyInLastMinutes OfHour** setting ensures that scale-down operations only happen in the last 10 minutes of the hour. These two settings enable you to optimize the use of your role instances based on the Windows Azure billing mechanism.

> *At the time of this writing, partial compute instance hours are billed as full compute hours for each clock hour an instance is deployed. For example, if you deploy a Small compute instance at 10:50 and delete the deployment at 11:10, then you will be billed for two Small compute hours, one compute hour for usage during 10:50 to 11:00 and another compute hour for usage during 11:00 to 11:10. Therefore, it makes sense to keep new instances alive for the remainder of the clock hour during which they were started. For more information, see "*Usage Charge Details for Windows Azure Bills.*"*

The two sets of settings interact with each other. In this example, scale-up operations are only allowed during the first 15 minutes of the hour. If the application block scales up a role a five minutes past the hour, the cool-down period will not allow any additional scale-up operations on that role for another 20 minutes. Because of the **scale UpOnlyInFirstMinutesOfHour** setting, this means that the stabilizer will not allow additional scale-up operations on this role within this clock hour.

Using the Planning Tool

This worksheet helps you to understand the interactions between different timing values that govern the overall autoscaling process. You can download this worksheet from the *Enterprise Library Community site* on CodePlex.

You can observe how different values can interact with each other by entering the values related to your environment.

Take the example in Figure 9 where Operands 1 and 2 are performance counters and Operand 3 is a custom business metric. You are evaluating the rules every 60 minutes.

Relevant Timing Option Inputs		Operands	
Timing ▼	**Minutes** ▼	**Operand name** ▼	**Aggregation Interval** ▼
Rule evaluation	60	Operand 1	25
Data collection	2	Operand 2	25
Log transfer	30	Operand 3	30
Cool down	20	Operand 4	0
		Operand 5	0
		Operand 6	0

FIGURE 9
Planning sheet inputs

The planning sheet shows the results in Figure 10.

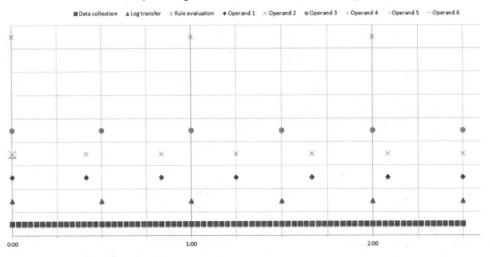

FIGURE 10
Planning results

This example demonstrates why you must be careful with your Autoscaling Application Block configuration settings. In the first hour, you can see how the timing of the data transfer means that you don't use the last values for Operands 1 and 2. You may decide to change the aggregation interval for the operands, change the log transfer interval, or decide that this behavior is appropriate for the data you collect from your application.

The real value of this tool becomes evident if you have a large number of operands.

The tool works by generating a set of data on a hidden sheet. If you unhide the worksheet, you will observe many #N/A values. These are deliberate and prevent the chart from showing jagged lines.

How the Autoscaling Application Block Works

This section summarizes how the Autoscaling Application Block works. If you're not interested in the internal workings of the block, you can skip this section. Figure 11 illustrates how the key components in the Autoscaling Application Block relate to each other, to Windows Azure, and to external components.

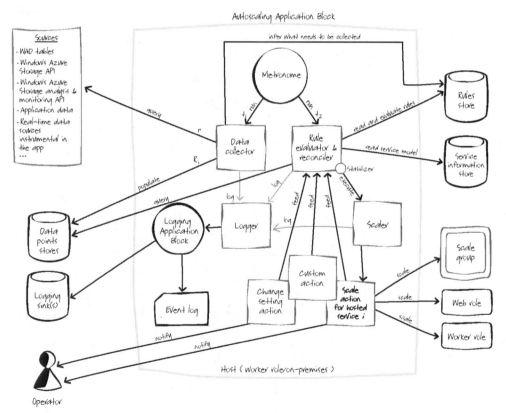

FIGURE 11
Overview of the Autoscaling Application Block

THE METRONOME

The work that the Autoscaling Application Block performs starts with the **Metronome**. The **Metronome** generates a "tick" count that enables it to run other activities on a regular schedule. In the Autoscaling Application Block, it runs each **Data Collector** activity every two minutes, the **Rule Evaluator** activity every t_1 seconds and the **Tracker** activity every t_2 seconds. The default value for t_1 is four minutes and for t_2 is five minutes, and you can override this in the application block's configuration settings.

THE DATA COLLECTORS

Before the Autoscaling Application Block can execute any reactive rules, it must collect the data point values from which it calculates the aggregate values used in the reactive rules. A data point is the value of a metric, such as CPU utilization, at a specific point in time. The **Data Collector** activities retrieve data points from your Windows Azure environment. The following table lists the possible sources of data points.

Monitoring Data Source	Description
Windows Azure Diagnostics tables	These are the tables that Windows Azure Diagnostics uses when it persists diagnostic data collected at run time from the Windows Azure environment. The block retrieves performance counter data from the **WADPerformance CountersTable**.
Windows Azure Storage API	The data collector can query your application's Windows Azure storage, including queues, blobs, and tables for custom data points. The block retrieves Windows Azure queue lengths using this API.
Windows Azure Storage Analytics API	The data collector can use this API to obtain data points related to your storage account, such as transaction statistics and capacity data.
Application data	The data collector can retrieve custom data points from your application. For example, the number of orders saved in a Windows Azure table.

The **Data Collector** activities write the data point values they collect to the **Data Points Store**.

Although not shown on the diagram, the application block creates the **Data Collector** activities after reading the **Rules Store** to determine the data points that the reactive rules will use. In effect, the application block infers which data points it should collect from the rule definitions in the rules store.

The service information store holds the information about your Windows Azure application that the **Data Collector** activities need to be able to access your roles and storage.

THE SERVICE INFORMATION STORE

The **Service Information Store** stores the service information for your Windows Azure application. This service information includes all of the information about your Windows Azure application that the block needs to be able to collect data points and perform scaling operations.

THE DATA POINTS STORE

The **Data Collector** activities populate the **Data Points Store**, which is populated with data points. The **Rule Evaluator** activity queries the **Data Points Store** for the data points that it needs to evaluate the reactive rules.

The block does not support hosting the Data Points Store in the local Windows Azure storage emulator. The block uses a Windows Azure API call that is not supported by the local storage emulator.

By default, the Autoscaling Application Block uses Windows Azure table storage for the **Data Points Store**.

THE RULE EVALUATOR

In addition to running the **Data Collector** activity, the **Metronome** also periodically runs the **Rule Evaluator** activity. When the **Rule Evaluator** task runs, it queries the **Rules Store** to discover which autoscaling rules it should apply at the current time. The **Rules Store** caches the rules in memory, but checks at a configurable period whether the rules have changed and if so, reloads the rules from the backing store. It then queries the data points in **Data Points Store** to calculate the aggregate values that it needs to evaluate the reactive rules. It also reconciles any conflicts between the rules before it executes the actions triggered by the rules.

For more information about how the application block reconciles conflicting rules and actions, see the topic "*Understanding Rule Ranks and Reconciliation.*"

THE RULES STORE

The **Rules Store** holds a list of all of the autoscaling rules that you have defined for your Windows Azure application. As a reminder, these rules can be constraint rules or reactive rules.

By default, the Autoscaling Application Block uses Windows Azure table storage for the **Rules Store**.

A rule can trigger one or more actions. The following table describes three types of actions that the Autoscaling Application Block supports.

Action type	Description
Scale action	Performs instance autoscaling or sends a notification to an operator.
Throttling action	Performs application throttling.
Custom action	Performs a custom, user-defined action.

The Autoscaling Application Block can also propose scaling actions to an operator via a notification mechanism.

THE LOGGER

The **Logger** component optionally uses the Enterprise Library Logging Application Block to save diagnostics information from the Autoscaling Application Block. You can also configure the **Logger** component to use other logging components such as the **System. Diagnostics** namespace.

For more information about the logging information that the application block generates, see the topic *"Autoscaling Application Block Logging"* on MSDN.

For more information about configuring the logger, see the topic *"Entering Configuration Information"* on MSDN.

THE SCALER

The **Scaler** is responsible for communicating with Windows Azure to add or remove role instances based on the rule actions. It also incorporates a stabilizer component to prevent the **Scaler** from repeatedly adding and removing role instances.

Scaling operations may take some time to complete. The **Scaler** initiates scaling operations and adds a message to the tracking queue to record the fact that the application block has requested a scaling operation.

The **Scaler** can send notification email messages to an operator detailing proposed scaling actions instead of performing the actions directly.

THE TRACKER

The **Tracker** activity tracks all the scaling operations initiated by the **Scaler**. The **Metronome** runs the **Tracker** activity by default every minute. The **Tracker** activity then checks to see which of the scaling operations in the tracking queue have completed successfully or failed. It logs details of completed scaling operations, including any error information if the operation failed, and then removes the entry from the queue.

More Information

For more information about design requirements, see "Building a Scalable, Multi-Tenant Application for Windows Azure" on MSDN:
http://msdn.microsoft.com/en-us/library/ff966483.aspx

For more information about compute hours in Windows Azure, see "Usage Charge Details for Windows Azure Bills":
http://go.microsoft.com/fwlink/?LinkID=234626

For more information about Windows Azure subscriptions, see the Windows Azure Support page:
http://www.microsoft.com/windowsazure/support/

For more information about how the Autoscaling Application Block reconciles conflicting rules, see "Understanding Rule Ranks and Reconciliation" on MSDN:
http://msdn.microsoft.com/en-us/library/hh680923(v=PandP.50).aspx

For a more detailed discussion of how you can estimate your Windows Azure running costs, see the chapter "How Much Will It Cost?" in the book "Moving Applications to the Cloud":
http://msdn.microsoft.com/en-us/library/ff803375.aspx

For a discussion of session state in Windows Azure applications, see "Storing Session State" in the book "Moving Applications to the Cloud":
http://msdn.microsoft.com/en-us/library/ff803373.aspx#sec11

For a discussion of some of the design issues associated with scalable worker roles, see "Scaling Applications by Using Worker Roles" in the book "Developing Applications for the Cloud":
http://msdn.microsoft.com/en-us/library/hh534484.aspx#sec14

For information about how you can use NuGet to prepare your Visual Studio project to work with the Autoscaling Application Block, see the topic "Adding the Autoscaling Application Block to a Host" on MSDN:
http://msdn.microsoft.com/en-us/library/hh680920(v=PandP.50).aspx

For information about how to host the Autoscaling Application Block in Windows Azure, see the topic "Hosting the Autoscaling Application Block in a Worker Role" on MSDN:
http://msdn.microsoft.com/en-us/library/hh680914(v=PandP.50).aspx

For information about how to reference the Enterprise Library assemblies, how Enterprise Library handles dependencies, and how to work with Enterprise Library objects, see "Using Enterprise Library in Applications" in the main Enterprise Library documentation on MSDN:
http://msdn.microsoft.com/en-us/library/ff664560(PandP.50).aspx

For information about how to host the Autoscaling Application Block in an on-premises application, see the topic "Hosting the Autoscaling Application Block in an On-Premises Application" on MSDN:
http://msdn.microsoft.com/en-us/library/hh680882(v=PandP.50).aspx

For more information about the code changes you must make in your Windows Azure application to enable it to save performance counter data, see the topic "Collecting Performance Counter Data" on MSDN:
http://msdn.microsoft.com/en-us/library/hh680886(v=PandP.50).aspx

You can also use the Windows Azure Diagnostics Configuration File (diagnostics.wadcfg) to configure your performance counters. For more details, see "How to Use the Windows Azure Diagnostics Configuration File" on MSDN:
http://go.microsoft.com/fwlink/?LinkID=234617

The Autoscaling Application Block rules can only operate on targets (roles and scale groups) that are identified in the block's service information. For more information, see the topic "Storing Your Service Information Data" on MSDN:
http://msdn.microsoft.com/en-us/library/hh680878(v=PandP.50).aspx

For information about a technique for parallelizing large calculations across multiple role instances, see the section "The Map Reduce Algorithm" in the book Developing Applications for the Cloud:
http://msdn.microsoft.com/en-us/library/ff966483.aspx#sec18

In Windows Azure, you can use the session state provider that stores session state in the shared cache. For more information, see the page "Session State Provider" on MSDN:
http://msdn.microsoft.com/en-us/library/gg185668.aspx

To minimize the risk of disclosing sensitive information, you should encrypt the contents of the service information store. For more information, see the topic "Encrypting the Rules Store and the Service Information Store" on MSDN:
http://msdn.microsoft.com/en-us/library/hh680910(v=PandP.50).aspx

For more information about how your Windows Azure application can detect a request for throttling behavior, see the topic "Implementing Throttling Behavior" on MSDN:
http://msdn.microsoft.com/en-us/library/hh680896(v=PandP.50).aspx

For information about how to define the throttling autoscaling rules, see the topic "Defining Throttling Autoscaling Rules" on MSDN:

http://msdn.microsoft.com/en-us/library/hh680908(v=PandP.50).aspx

For a complete example of how the Tailspin Surveys application uses throttling behavior, see Chapter 5, "Making Tailspin Surveys More Elastic" in this guide.

If your reactive rules use performance counter data from your Windows Azure application, you must make sure that your application transfers the performance counter data that the rules consume to Windows Azure Diagnostics storage. For an example of how to do this, see the section "Collecting Performance Counter Data from Tailspin Surveys" in Chapter 5, "Making Tailspin Surveys More Elastic" of this guide.

For information about the logging data that the Autoscaling Application Block generates, see the topic "Autoscaling Application Block Logging" on MSDN:
http://msdn.microsoft.com/en-us/library/hh680883(v=PandP.50).aspx

For more information about reading and parsing the Autoscaling Application Block log messages, see the topic "Reading the Autoscaling Application Block Log Messages":
http://msdn.microsoft.com/en-us/library/hh680909(v=PandP.50).aspx

For more information about configuring the Autoscaling Application Block and configuring the logger, see the topic "Entering Configuration Information" on MSDN:
http://msdn.microsoft.com/en-us/library/hh680915(v=PandP.50).aspx

For more information about reading from the rules store, see the "IRulesStore interface" in the API documentation on MSDN:
http://go.microsoft.com/fwlink/?LinkID=234680

For more information about reading from the service information store, see the "IServiceInformationStore interface" in the API documentation on MSDN:
http://go.microsoft.com/fwlink/?LinkID=234681

For more information about reading from the rules store, see the "IDataPointsStore interface" in the API documentation on MSDN:
http://go.microsoft.com/fwlink/?LinkID=234682

For a complete example of using the different data sources to visualize the Autoscaling Application Block activities, see the section "Visualizing the Autoscaling Actions" in Chapter 5, "Making Tailspin Surveys More Elastic."

For more information about how to configure notifications, see the topic "Using Notifications and Manual Scaling" on MSDN:
http://msdn.microsoft.com/en-us/library/hh680885(v=PandP.50).aspx

For more information extending and modifying the Autoscaling Application Block, see the topic "Extending and Modifying the Autoscaling Application Block" on MSDN:
http://msdn.microsoft.com/en-us/library/hh680889(v=PandP.50).aspx

- For more information about custom actions, see the topic "Creating a Custom Action" on MSDN:
  http://msdn.microsoft.com/en-us/library/hh680921(v=PandP.50).aspx

- For an example of a custom action and a custom operand, see Chapter 5, "Making Tailspin Surveys More Elastic."

- For more information about custom operands, see the topic "Creating a Custom Operand" on MSDN:
  http://msdn.microsoft.com/en-us/library/hh680912(v=PandP.50).aspx

- For more information about creating a custom rules store, see the topic "Creating a Custom Rules Store" on MSDN:
  http://msdn.microsoft.com/en-us/library/hh680933(v=PandP.50).aspx

- For more information about creating a custom service information store, see the topic "Creating a Custom Service Information Store" on MSDN:
  http://msdn.microsoft.com/en-us/library/hh680884(v=PandP.50).aspx

- For more information about creating a custom logger, see the topic "Creating a Custom Logger" on MSDN:
  http://msdn.microsoft.com/en-us/library/hh680926(v=PandP.50).aspx

For more information about extending the Enterprise Library, see the "Extensibility Hands-on Labs for Microsoft Enterprise Library 5.0":
http://go.microsoft.com/fwlink/?LinkId=209184

For more information about the WASABiCmdlets, see the topic "Using the WASABiCmdlets Windows PowerShell Cmdlets" on MSDN:
http://msdn.microsoft.com/en-us/library/hh680938(v=PandP.50).aspx

For more information about the Windows Azure PowerShell Cmdlets, see "Windows Azure PowerShell Cmdlets" on CodePlex:
http://wappowershell.codeplex.com/

For more information about SCOM, see "System Center Operations Manager" on TechNet:
http://technet.microsoft.com/en-us/systemcenter/om/default.aspx

For more information about writing autoscaling rules, see the topics
"Defining Constraint Rules" and "Defining Reactive Rules" on
MSDN:

http://msdn.microsoft.com/en-us/library/hh680917(v=PandP.50).aspx
http://msdn.microsoft.com/en-us/library/hh680897(v=PandP.50).aspx

For more information about billing details in Windows Azure, see
"Usage Charge Details for Windows Azure Bills":
http://go.microsoft.com/fwlink/?LinkID=234626

The Autoscale Planner worksheet helps you to understand the
interactions between different timing values that govern the overall
autoscaling process. You can download this worksheet from the
Enterprise Library Community site on CodePlex:
http://go.microsoft.com/fwlink/?LinkID=234704

To access web resources more easily, see the online version of the
bibliography on MSDN:
http://msdn.microsoft.com/en-us/library/hh749032(v=PandP.50).aspx

5   Making Tailspin Surveys More Elastic

This chapter walks you through the changes that Tailspin made when it added the Autoscaling Application Block to the Surveys application. These changes made it possible to automate the processes of adding and removing role instances as well as to manage the application's resource requirements in response to changes in demand for the application. The chapter also shows how Tailspin configured different sets of autoscaling rules for different elements of the Surveys application to meet their different autoscaling requirements and describes how Tailspin plans to monitor and refine its autoscaling rules.

The Premise

The number of customers using the Tailspin Surveys application continues to grow, with customers creating and publishing surveys all around the world. The number of surveys with large numbers of respondents is also increasing. Tailspin has noticed that there are an increasing number of bursts in demand associated with these large surveys, with the bursts occurring very shortly after the customer publishes the survey. Tailspin cannot predict when these bursts will occur, or in which geographic location they will occur. Tailspin has also noticed that there are overall bursts in demand at particular times in particular geographic locations. For some of these bursts Tailspin understands the cause, such as an upcoming holiday season; for others, Tailspin does not yet understand what triggered the burst in demand.

The Tailspin operators have always carefully monitored the traffic and the utilization levels of their systems. When needed, they manually adjust the number of web and worker role instances to accommodate the change in demand. However, they find it difficult to determine the correct number of role instances to have active at specific times. To ensure high performance and availability for the Surveys application, they usually start up more servers than they

might need. However, when a large burst in traffic occurs, it can take Tailspin's operators some time to react and increase the server capacity, especially for non-US based data centers. Also, operators at Tailspin have sometimes been slow to shut down servers when a burst in activity is over.

The result of this manual process is that there are often too many active role instances, both during times of normal activity and during bursts of activity, which increases the operational costs of the Surveys application. Also, when an unpredicted burst in traffic occurs, it can take too long to add new role instances, which results in poor performance and a negative user experience.

Goals and Requirements

Tailspin wants to make their application more elastic, so that the number of servers can grow and shrink automatically as demand varies. This will reduce the costs of running the Surveys application in Windows Azure™ technology platform and also reduce the number of ad hoc, manual tasks for Tailspin's operators.

Tailspin wants to set explicit boundaries on the number of active role instances, to keep the operational costs within a predictable range and to ensure that the Windows Azure SLA applies to the Surveys application.

In the past, Tailspin has encountered some very sudden bursts in demand; for example, when customers have offered a reward for the first number of people to complete a survey. Tailspin is concerned that new role instances cannot be started fast enough to meet these types of activity bursts. In this type of scenario, Tailspin would like to be able to immediately begin degrading some of the non-essential functionality of the application so that the UI response times are maintained until the new role instances have started and are available to help out. Tailspin would also like its operators to be notified by an SMS message when certain scaling operations are taking place.

> Currently, all of Tailspin's operators are based in the United States (US), so the number of operators on duty is lower outside of normal working hours. As a result, they sometimes don't respond immediately to bursts in demand in other geographic locations.
>
> We need to reduce the operational costs to be more competitive. By using autoscaling in the Surveys application, we can do that and still meet our service-level agreement (SLA) requirements.

> In the Tailspin Surveys application, the number of role instances is the key resource that Tailspin can vary to meet changes in workload. In other applications, the resources could include items such as the number of queues, or the size of the database.

Tailspin can already predict when some bursts in demand will occur based on data that it has collected in the past. Tailspin wants to be able to pre-emptively timetable the addition and removal of role instances so that there is no lag when such a burst in demand occurs.

Overall, Tailspin wants to reduce the operational costs while still providing the maximum performance for their end users. This means using the minimum number of role instances required to perform a task at the required level of performance. When the values for certain performance counters, such as CPU usage, exceed a predefined threshold, the system should add more role instances until the values have dropped to more acceptable levels. When the values for these performance counters drop enough, the role instance should be removed again.

We conducted performance tests to identify the most resource-intensive areas of our application. It turned out that some of these areas could be turned off or postponed to reduce the load on our application.

Tailspin must be able to control the autoscaling parameters by defining rules. A rule defines which instances will be scaled, which metrics to monitor, and what thresholds to use for scaling up and down. For example, when CPU utilization hits 80% as averaged across the running instances, add a new role instance. It should also be possible to use rules to set the minimum and maximum number of role instances for a certain timeframe. These rules should be configurable through a user interface.

It is difficult to determine the right number of role instances for a particular task, even with an automatic scaling solution. Tailspin wants to have access to detailed logging information that records the autoscaling activities that have taken place. For example, Tailspin wants to know when a role instance was added or removed and what triggered that action. Tailspin plans to analyze this data and use the results to refine the autoscaling behavior of the Surveys application.

Tailspin wants to get an overview of the resource utilization over time. For example, it wants to know how many role instances were active at a certain point in time, what their CPU utilization was, and how many concurrent users were active at that time. Tailspin wants to be able to analyze when bursts in overall demand occurred in particular geographic locations so that it can plan for these events in the future. Tailspin also plans to use this information to fine-tune their pricing strategy based on more detailed analysis of predicted levels of demand.

Tailspin has deployed the Surveys application to multiple Windows Azure data centers to ensure that the Surveys application is available in a data center located close to the majority of people who complete surveys. Tailspin would like to use a single management application from which Tailspin can create and edit the various autoscaling rules used in the different geographical locations, and also monitor the autoscaling behavior in all the data centers. At the same time, Tailspin wants to minimize the costs of this distributed autoscaling solution.

Overview of the Autoscaling Solution

This section describes how the Autoscaling Application Block helped the Tailspin Surveys application become more elastic.

USING THE AUTOSCALING APPLICATION BLOCK IN TAILSPIN SURVEYS

This section describes how the Surveys application uses the features of the Autoscaling Application Block.

For more information about autoscaling and how the Autoscaling Application Block works, see Chapter 4, "Autoscaling and Windows Azure," in this guide.

Features of the Autoscaling Application Block

The Autoscaling Application Block provides two types of autoscaling rules: constraint rules and reactive rules. Tailspin uses both types of rules in the Surveys application.

Tailspin uses constraint rules to specify minimum and maximum numbers of role instances for both its worker and web roles. Tailspin can set minimum values to ensure that it meets its SLA commitments and use the maximum values to ensure that its costs are kept under control. It uses a number of constraint rules to set different maximum and minimum values at different times of the day when it can predict changes in the workload for the Surveys application.

Tailspin uses reactive rules to enable the Surveys application to respond to sudden changes in demand. These rules are based on metrics that Tailspin has identified for the Surveys application. Some of these metrics are standard performance counters; some require custom data that is specific to the Tailspin Surveys application.

In addition to rules that automatically change the number of role instances in the Surveys application, Tailspin also uses reactive rules to modify the behavior of the application. These rules are designed to help the surveys application respond quickly to sudden bursts in demand before new role instances can be started.

Tailspin operators also regularly review all of the diagnostics data that is collected from the Surveys application in order to ensure that the current rules provide the optimum behavior, that Tailspin's SLAs are being met, and that there are no unnecessary role instances running. Tailspin operators use this data to refine the set of rules in order to better meet the SLA and cost requirements of the Surveys application.

For more information about the functionality and usage of the Autoscaling Application Block, see Chapter 4, "*Autoscaling and Windows Azure.*"

Hosting the Autoscaling Application Block in Tailspin Surveys

Tailspin decided to host the Autoscaling Application Block in a web role in Windows Azure. It also considered hosting the Autoscaling Application Block in an on-premises application. Tailspin did not identify any benefits from hosting the Autoscaling Application Block in an on-premises application; it has no plans to integrate the Autoscaling Application Block with any existing on-premises logging or diagnostic tools. The following diagram shows some of the high-level components of the Tailspin Surveys application that will take part in the autoscaling process.

The Tailspin autoscaling hosted service includes the autoscaling management web role and the autoscaling worker role. These two roles are typically developed together, and it simplifies the deployment of the Surveys application to place them in the same hosted service.

If your management website has more responsibilities than managing the autoscaling process, you should consider using a separate hosted service for each role so they can be developed and deployed in isolation.

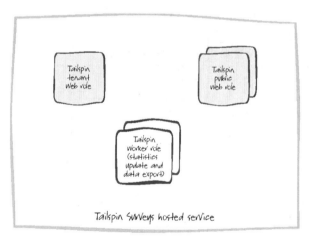

FIGURE 1
Components that take part in autoscaling in Tailspin Surveys

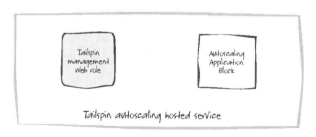

In the Tailspin Surveys application, the public web role that people use to submit survey answers and the worker role will benefit from scaling; both have been affected by high usage levels in the past. Tailspin does not anticipate that the tenant's web roles will be affected by high levels of demand because tenants use the tenant web role to design new surveys. However, Tailspin will add some autoscaling rules in case of any unexpected bursts in demand.

Scale Groups in Tailspin Surveys

The Tailspin Surveys application only has two role types that Tailspin wants to scale automatically: the public web role and the worker role responsible for statistics calculation and data export. These two roles have different usage patterns and need different autoscaling rules, so there is no benefit in grouping them together in a scale group. Similarly, the instances of each role type that run in different Windows Azure data centers also need to be scaled independently of each other. Therefore, Tailspin does not use the scale groups feature of the Autoscaling Application Block.

> One of the reasons Tailspin designed the Surveys application with multiple web roles was because of the differences in anticipated usage patterns. Each web and worker role can be scaled independently of the others.

AUTOSCALING RULES IN TAILSPIN SURVEYS

The following table shows the initial set of constraint rules that Tailspin identified for use in the Surveys application.

> Tailspin has been careful to ensure that the tenant and management web roles can be scaled in case they need to add autoscaling behavior to these roles in the future.

Description	Rank	Timetable	Role	Maximum instances	Minimum instances
Default constraints for all roles	0	All day, every day	Tailspin worker role	5	2
Default constraints for all roles	0	All day, every day	Tailspin public web role	5	2
Default constraints for all roles	0	All day, every day	Tailspin tenant web role	5	2
Additional instances for public web during peak hours	5	8:00 – 9:50 on Monday, Tuesday, Wednesday, Thursday, Friday	Tailspin public web role	6	3

The following table shows the initial set of reactive rules that Tailspin identified for use in the Surveys application.

Description	Target	Action
Look at number of rejected requests and CPU usage for the public website. If both becomes too large, then scale up the number of instances.	Tailspin Surveys public web role	Add one instance
Look at number of rejected requests and CPU usage for the public website. If both drop to acceptable levels, then reduce the number of instances.	Tailspin Surveys public web role	Remove one instance
When there is a burst in activity on the tenant website or the worker role, then enable throttling. This should reduce the load so that the site remains workable. If the load remains high, then the scaling rules will kick in and increase the number of instances.	Tailspin Surveys worker role Tailspin Surveys tenant web role	Throttling mode "ReduceSystemLoad"
When the burst in activity is over, then disable throttling.	Tailspin Surveys worker role Tailspin Surveys tenant web role	Throttling mode "Normal"
When there are many tenants or surveys and there is high CPU usage, then add more capacity to the public web site.	Tailspin Surveys public web role	Add one instance
When there are a normal number of tenants and surveys, then decrease the number of instances.	Tailspin Surveys public web role	Remove one instance
Look at number of rejected requests and CPU for the tenant website. If either becomes too large, then scale up the number of instances.	Tailspin Surveys tenant web role	Add one instance

The minimum values are important for Tailspin to meet its SLA commitments; the maximum values help Tailspin to manage the costs of running the Surveys application.

Look at number of rejected requests and CPU for the tenant website. If the load is acceptable, then reduce the number of instances.	Tailspin Surveys tenant web role	Remove one instance

These tables show the initial set of rules that Tailspin used in the production version of the Surveys application. Tailspin will monitor and evaluate these rules to determine if they are producing optimal scaling behavior. Tailspin expects to make the following types of adjustment to the set of rules to improve their effectiveness.

- Modify the threshold values that determine when to scale down or out and when to enable or disable throttling.
- Add additional constraint rules to handle other predictable changes in activity.
- Change the metrics and timespans that the reactive rules use to trigger scaling actions.
- Use different rule sets in different Windows Azure data centers to reflect different usage patterns in different geographic locations.

From the initial set of rules, Tailspin identified a set of metrics that it must configure the application block to collect. The following table shows the initial set of metrics that Tailspin identified for the reactive rules in the Surveys application.

Description	Aggregate function	Timespan	Source	Metric
CPU usage in the Surveys public web role	Average	20 minutes	Tailspin public web role	\Processor (_Total)\% Processor Time
CPU usage in the Surveys worker role	Average	5 minutes	Tailspin worker role	\Processor (_Total)\% Processor Time
CPU usage in the Surveys tenant web role	Average	20 minutes	Tailspin tenant web role	\Processor (_Total)\% Processor Time
CPU usage in the Surveys tenant web role	Average	5 minutes	Tailspin tenant web role	\Processor (_Total)\% Processor Time

Rejected ASP. NET requests in the Surveys public web role	Average	10 minutes	Tailspin public web role	\ASP.NET\ Requests Rejected
Rejected ASP. NET requests in the Surveys tenant web role	Average	10 minutes	Tailspin tenant web role	\ASP.NET\ Requests Rejected
Number of surveys submitted	Average	10 minutes	The Surveys application	The number of active surveys in the Surveys application
Number of tenants	Average	10 minutes	The Surveys application	The number of registered tenants
Number of instances of the Surveys public web role.	Last	8 minutes	Tailspin public web role	Role instance count

Tailspin developed custom operands to collect the number of active surveys and active tenants from the Surveys application.

COLLECTING AUTOSCALING HISTORY DATA IN TAILSPIN SURVEYS

Tailspin knows that usage patterns for the Surveys application change over time in different geographical locations. Tailspin is also aware that through careful analysis of the way the Surveys application is used, it can identify usage patterns.

Analyzing past behavior helps you to optimize your autoscaling rules.

Tailspin prefers to be proactive in the way that it approaches autoscaling, so it favors constraint rules over reactive rules. In this way it can try to ensure that it has the right number of instances active so that it can meet its SLA commitments without the need to add new instances in response to changes in workload. Therefore, every month Tailspin reviews the log data collected from the Autoscaling Application Block to try to identify any new patterns or changes in existing patterns. If there are any changes to usage patterns, it either modifies existing constraint rules or adds new ones.

Tailspin still maintains a set of reactive rules so that the Surveys application can respond to any unanticipated changes in its workload. Tailspin also analyzes when and why these reactive rules ran to make sure that they are performing the optimum scaling operations.

Tailspin's administrators do not need to be able to edit the other elements, such as the subscription details and the list of scalable roles in the service information definition. These values are set once when the application is first deployed to Windows Azure.

AN AUTOSCALING CONFIGURATION UI

Although it is possible for administrators to edit the XML file that contains Tailspin's autoscaling rules directly, this is a potentially error-prone process. If used, a schema-aware XML editor may handle some of the validation issues, but some values in the rules definition file refer to entries in the service information definition and any errors in the references will not be detected by the XML validation. In addition, the administrators would also need to upload the rules XML file to the correct storage location for the application block to be able to load and use the new rules definitions. Because of these challenges, Tailspin decided to build a web-hosted rules editor that would handle all of the validation issues and be able to save the rules to the correct location.

There are similar issues associated with the XML file that contains the Survey's service information description. Tailspin anticipates that administrators will need to edit the scale group definitions in this file, and wants administrators to be able to perform this task through the same UI that they use for editing rules.

NOTIFYING OPERATORS BY SMS WHEN A SCALING OPERATION TAKES PLACE

Sending notifications by SMS when performing a scaling action is not one of the built-in features of the Autoscaling Application Block. Tailspin decided to create a custom action to send SMS notifications. Tailspin can add this custom action to selected reactive rules so that its operators are always notified when significant scaling operations are taking place.

Although the Autoscaling Application Block already includes a feature that can send notifications when it performs a scaling action, the built-in feature uses email and Tailspin prefers to use SMS messages to notify its operators.

Inside the Implementation

This section describes some of the details of how Tailspin hosted the Autoscaling Application Block and modified the Surveys application to work with the application block. If you are not interested in the details, you can skip to the next section.

You may find it useful to have the Tailspin solution open in Microsoft® Visual Studio® development system while you read this section so that you can refer to the code directly.

For instructions about how to install the Tailspin Surveys application, see Appendix B, "Tailspin Surveys Installation Guide."

ENABLING THE AUTOSCALING APPLICATION BLOCK TO READ FROM THE .CSCFG FILE

The Autoscaling Application Block reads connection string information from the .cscfg file in order to access Windows Azure storage. It does this by using the **FromConfigurationSetting** method in the **CloudStorageAccount** class. For this to work, the Surveys application must set up a configuration setting publisher at startup. The following code from the Global.asax.cs file in the **Tailspin.Web.Management** project shows this.

C#
```
CloudStorageAccount.SetConfigurationSettingPublisher(
  (s, p) => p(RoleEnvironment.GetConfigurationSettingValue(s)));
```

For more information, see *"CloudStorageAccount.SetConfigurationSettingPublisher Method"* on MSDN.

> You should set up a configuration setting publisher for each role that the Autoscaling Application Block is configured to monitor and scale.

TAILSPIN'S SERVICE INFORMATION DEFINITION

The following code snippet shows the default service information definition for the Tailspin Surveys application. Tailspin defines the contents of this file once for the initial deployment; they do not anticipate changing anything after the Autoscaling Application Block is running.

XML
```
<serviceModel ...>
  <subscriptions>
    <!--
      Todo when installing the RI for the first time:
      Update your subscription ID and Certificate Thumbprint
    -->
    <subscription name="TailspinSubscription"
                  subscriptionId="[Enter subscription id here]"
                  certificateThumbprint="
                  [Enter certificate thumbprint here]"
                  certificateStoreName="My"
                  certificateStoreLocation="LocalMachine">
      <services>
        <service dnsPrefix="Tailspin-Surveys"
        slot="Staging" scalingMode="Scale">
          <roles>
            <role alias="SurveyWorkers"
                  roleName="Tailspin.Workers.Surveys"
                  wadStorageAccountName="TailspinStorage" />
            <role alias="PublicWebSite"
                  roleName="Tailspin.Web.Survey.Public"
```

```
                                wadStorageAccountName="TailspinStorage" />
                    <role alias="TenantWebSite"
                          roleName="Tailspin.Web"
                          wadStorageAccountName="TailspinStorage" />
                </roles>
              </service>
            </services>
            <storageAccounts>
              <!--
                Todo when installing the RI for the first time:
                Update the connection string to your storage account
              -->
              <storageAccount alias="TailspinStorage"
                              connectionString=
                              "[Enter connection string here]">
                <queues>
                  <queue alias="SurveyAnswerStoredQueue"
                         queueName="surveyanswerstored" />
                  <queue alias="SurveyTransferQueue"
                         queueName="surveytransfer" />
                </queues>
              </storageAccount>
            </storageAccounts>
          </subscription>
        </subscriptions>
        <scaleGroups />
        <stabilizer scaleUpCooldown="00:10:00"
                    scaleDownCooldown="00:10:00"
            notificationsCooldown="00:30:00">
          <role roleAlias="PublicWebSite" scaleUpCooldown="00:08:00"
            scaleDownCooldown="00:15:00" />
        </stabilizer>
      </serviceModel>
```

Tailspin is only using the Autoscaling Application Block to scale three roles, so it is not using scale groups. If you use scale groups in your application, you define them in the service information definition file.

If you are installing the Tailspin Surveys application, you must edit this file to add the information that is specific to your Windows Azure account. For more information, see the section "Setup and Physical Deployment" in this chapter. A sample service information definition file is included in the "Sample Stores" folder in the Visual Studio solution.

The role and queue aliases are used in Tailspin Survey's autoscaling rules.

The **stabilizer** element shows the cool-down periods configured by Tailspin. These include global settings and specific settings for the public website. Tailspin has extended to 15 minutes the amount of time that must elapse after a scaling operation before the public website can be scaled down. Scaling up the public website can happen slightly earlier than the other roles.

TAILSPIN'S AUTOSCALING RULES

The following code snippets show a default set of rules that Tailspin used when it first started using the Autoscaling Application Block. Tailspin plans to evaluate the effectiveness of these rules in scaling the Surveys application, and will make changes when it has collected sufficient data to be able to analyze the autoscaling behavior in their production environment. Tailspin has built a web-based rule editor to enable operators to edit the rules more easily. For more information about Tailspin's web-based rule editor, see the section "Editing and Saving Rules" in this chapter.

Tailspin Surveys Constraint Rules

The following code snippet shows the initial set of constraint rules that Tailspin configured for the Surveys application. There is a default rule that sets default values for all of the roles in Tailspin Surveys; it has a rank of zero. The second rule scales up the Tailspin Surveys worker role in anticipation of greater levels of activity during the work week.

XML

```
<rules ...>
  <constraintRules>
    <rule name="Default constraints for all roles"
          description="This rule sets the default constraints for
          all web and worker roles. The minimum values guard our
          SLA, by ensuring there will never be less than these
          instances. The maximum values guard our wallet, by
          ensuring there will never be more than the configured
          number of instances."
          enabled="true" rank="0">
      <timetable startTime="00:00:00"
                 duration="1.00:00:00" utcOffset="+00:00">
        <daily />
      </timetable>
      <actions>
        <range target="SurveyWorkers" min="2" max="5" />
```

```
            <range target="PublicWebSite" min="2" max="5" />
            <range target="TenantWebSite" min="2" max="5" />
        </actions>
    </rule>
    <rule name="Additional instances for public web during peak
          hours" description="Our testing has indicated that
          there will be additional load during peak hours. To
          accommodate for that additional load, there will be
          additional instances for the public website. These
          peaks occur during working hours and early evenings.
          By providing a higher rank, this rule takes precedence
          over the default rule."
          enabled="true" rank="5">
        <timetable startTime="08:00:00" duration="09:50:00"
                utcOffset="+00:00">
            <weekly days="Monday Tuesday Wednesday Thursday Friday" />
        </timetable>
        <actions>
            <range target="PublicWebSite" min="3" max="6" />
        </actions>
    </rule>
  </constraintRules>
  ...
</rules>
```

Tailspin Surveys Reactive Scaling Rules

The following snippet shows how Tailspin initially defined the reactive scaling rules for the Surveys application. The first pair of rules defines how the Surveys public web role should scale up or down based on the number of rejected ASP.NET requests and CPU utilization levels. The second pair of rules defines how the Surveys public web role should scale up or down based on the number of tenants and active surveys. The third pair of rules defines how the Surveys tenant web role should scale up or down based on the number of rejected ASP.NET requests and CPU utilization levels.

Notice how the reactive rules are paired; one specifies when to scale up, and one specifies when to scale down.

XML
```
<rules ...>
  ...
  <reactiveRules>
  ...
    <rule name="Public Web - Heavy Demand (Increase)"
          description="Look at number of rejected requests and
          CPU for the public website. If either becomes too
          large, then scale up the number of instances."
```

```
       enabled="true">
  <actions>
    <scale target="PublicWebSite" by="1" />
  </actions>
  <when>
    <all>
      <greater operand=
       "PublicWeb_AspNetRequestsRejected_Avg_10m" than="5" />
      <greater operand="PublicWeb_CPU_Avg_20m" than="80" />
    </all>
  </when>
</rule>
<rule name="Public Web - Normal Demand (Reduce)"
      description="Look at number of rejected requests and
      CPU for the public website. If both drop to acceptable
      levels, then reduce the number of instances."
      enabled="true">
  <actions>
    <scale target="PublicWebSite" by="-1" />
  </actions>
  <when>
    <all>
      <lessOrEqual operand=
       "PublicWeb_AspNetRequestsRejected_Avg_10m" than="1" />
      <lessOrEqual operand="PublicWeb_CPU_Avg_20m" than="40" />
    </all>
  </when>
</rule>

<rule name="PublicWeb - Many Tenants Or Surveys (Increase)"
      description="When there are many tenants or surveys and
      the CPU usage is high, then we'll need more capacity in
      the public website. This rule demonstrates
      the use of the custom operands, called ActiveSurveyCount
      and TenantCount. Using the load simulation page, you can
      easily add and remove tenants and surveys to test the
      load on the system."
      enabled="true">
  <actions>
    <scale target="PublicWebSite" by="1" />
  </actions>
  <when>
    <all>
      <any>
        <greaterOrEqual operand=
```

```
                "Tailspin_ActiveSurveyCount_Avg_10m"
                        than="50 * PublicWeb_InstanceCount_Last" />
            <greaterOrEqual operand="Tailspin_TenantCount_Avg_10m"
                        than="50 * PublicWeb_InstanceCount_Last" />
        </any>
        <greater operand="PublicWeb_CPU_Avg_20m" than="50"/>
      </all>
    </when>
  </rule>
  <rule name="PublicWeb - Normal Tenants And Surveys (Decrease)"
        description="When there are a normal number of tenants and surveys, then
        decrease the number of instances."
        enabled="true">
    <actions>
      <scale target="PublicWebSite" by="-1" />
    </actions>
    <when>
      <all>
        <less operand="Tailspin_TenantCount_Avg_10m"
              than="30 * PublicWeb_InstanceCount_Last" />
        <less operand="Tailspin_ActiveSurveyCount_Avg_10m"
              than="30 * PublicWeb_InstanceCount_Last" />
      </all>
    </when>
  </rule>

  <rule name="TenantWeb - Heavy demand (Increase)"
        description="Look at number of rejected requests and
        CPU for the tenant website. If either becomes too
        large, then scale up the number of instances."
        enabled="true">
    <actions>
      <scale target="TenantWebSite" by="1" />
    </actions>
    <when>
      <all>
        <greaterOrEqual operand="TenantWeb_AspNetRequestsRejected_avg_10m"
                        than="5" />
        <greaterOrEqual operand="TenantWeb_CPU_Avg_20m" than="80" />
      </all>
    </when>
  </rule>
  <rule name="TenantWeb - Normal Demand (Decrease)"
        description="Look at number of rejected requests and
        CPU for the tenant website. If the load is acceptable,
```

```
              then reduce the number of instances."
              enabled="true">
       <actions>
         <scale target="TenantWebSite" by="-1" />
       </actions>
       <when>
         <all>
<lessOrEqual operand=
    "TenantWeb_AspNetRequestsRejected_avg_10m" than="2" />
<lessOrEqual operand=
    "TenantWeb_CPU_Avg_20m" than="60"/>
</all>
       </when>
     </rule>
    ...
  </reactiveRules>
  ...
</rules>
```

Tailspin has not assigned a rank to any of the reactive rules.

Tailspin Surveys Reactive Throttling Rules

Tailspin uses throttling rules to dynamically change the behavior of the Surveys public web role. It uses CPU utilization to determine when to enable and when to disable throttling in the Surveys application.

Throttling behavior is triggered by using the **changeSetting** action.

For more information about how Tailspin implemented the throttling behavior in the Surveys application, see the section "Implementing Throttling Behavior," later in this chapter.

XML
```
<rules ...>
  ...
  <reactiveRules>
    ...

<rule name=
    "TenantWeb &amp; Survey Worker - Burst - Throttle"
         description="When there is a burst in activity on the
         tenant website and the worker role, then enable
         throttling. This should reduce the load so that the
         site remains workable. If the load remains high, then
         the scaling rules will kick in and increase the number
         of instances. Throttling in Tailspin does the
         following:
```

```
                 * Disable exporting of values to Microsoft SQL Server
                   in the worker role.
                 * Only allow paying tenants to the tenant site. Tenants
                   on a trial subscription cannot enter."
                 enabled="true">
          <actions>
            <changeSetting target="SurveyWorkers"
settingName="ThrottlingMode"
                           value="ReduceSystemLoad" />
            <changeSetting target="TenantWebSite"
settingName="ThrottlingMode"
                           value="ReduceSystemLoad" />
          </actions>
          <when>
            <all>
              <greaterOrEqual operand="TenantWeb_CPU_Avg_5m" than="90" />
              <greaterOrEqual operand="SurveyWorkers_CPU_Avg_5m" than="90" />
            </all>
          </when>
        </rule>
        <rule name="TenantWeb &amp; Survey Worker - Burst - Stop throttling"
          description="When there is no burst in activity, then
          disable throttling."
          enabled="true">
          <actions>
            <changeSetting target="TenantWebSite" settingName="ThrottlingMode"
                           value="Normal" />
            <changeSetting target="SurveyWorkers" settingName="ThrottlingMode"
                           value="Normal" />
          </actions>
          <when>
            <any>
              <lessOrEqual operand="SurveyWorkers_CPU_Avg_5m" than="50" />
              <lessOrEqual operand="TenantWeb_CPU_Avg_5m" than="50" />
            </any>
          </when>
        </rule>
        ...
      </reactiveRules>
      ...
    </rules>
```

Tailspin Surveys Operands

In addition to using the built-in performance counter operands, Tailspin created two custom operands, **activeSurveysOperand** and **tenantCountOperand**, that enable it to use the number of surveys with more than a specified number of answers in a rule and the number of tenants.

XML

```xml
<rules ...>
  ...
  <operands>
    <roleInstanceCount alias="PublicWeb_InstanceCount_Last" timespan="00:08:00"
      aggregate="Last" role="PublicWebSite" />
    <performanceCounter alias="PublicWeb_AspNetRequestsRejected_Avg_10m"
        timespan="00:10:00" aggregate="Average" source="PublicWebSite"
        performanceCounterName="\ASP.NET\Requests Rejected" />
    <performanceCounter alias="PublicWeb_CPU_Avg_20m" timespan="00:20:00"
        aggregate="Average" source="PublicWebSite"
        performanceCounterName="\Processor(_Total)\% Processor Time" />
    <activeSurveysOperand alias="Tailspin_ActiveSurveyCount_Avg_10m"
        timespan="00:10:00" aggregate="Average" minNumberOfAnswers="0"
        xmlns="http://Tailspin/ActiveSurveys" />
    <tenantCountOperand alias="Tailspin_TenantCount_Avg_10m" timespan="00:10:00"
        aggregate="Average" xmlns="http://Tailspin/TenantCount" />
    <performanceCounter alias="TenantWeb_AspNetRequestsRejected_avg_10m"
        timespan="00:10:00" aggregate="Average" source="TenantWebSite"
        performanceCounterName="\ASP.NET\Requests Rejected" />
    <performanceCounter alias="TenantWeb_CPU_Avg_20m" timespan="00:20:00"
        aggregate="Average" source="TenantWebSite"
        performanceCounterName="\Processor(_Total)\% Processor Time" />
    <performanceCounter alias="SurveyWorkers_CPU_Avg_5m" timespan="00:05:00"
        aggregate="Average" source="SurveyWorkers"
        performanceCounterName="\Processor(_Total)\% Processor Time" />
    <performanceCounter alias="TenantWeb_CPU_Avg_5m" timespan="00:05:00"
        aggregate="Average" source="TenantWebSite"
        performanceCounterName="\Processor(_Total)\% Processor Time" />
  </operands>
</rules>
```

For more information about how Tailspin implemented the custom operands, see the section "Implementing Custom Operands" in this chapter.

You must remember to modify your application to collect the performance counter data that your reactive rules use and to transfer the performance counter data to Windows Azure storage.

COLLECTING PERFORMANCE COUNTER DATA FROM TAILSPIN SURVEYS

The reactive rules that Tailspin uses for the Surveys application use performance counter data from the public web role and worker role. The Autoscaling Application Block expects to find this performance counter data in the Windows Azure Diagnostics table named **WAD PerformanceCountersTable** in Windows Azure storage. Tailspin modified the public web and worker role in the Surveys application to save the performance counter data that the application block uses to evaluate the reactive rules.

The following code sample from the **WebRole** class in the Tailspin public web role configures the role to collect and save performance counter data.

```csharp
C#
...
using Microsoft.WindowsAzure;
using Microsoft.WindowsAzure.Diagnostics;
using Microsoft.WindowsAzure.ServiceRuntime;

public class WebRole : RoleEntryPoint
{
    public override bool OnStart()
{
var config =
    DiagnosticMonitor.GetDefaultInitialConfiguration();

        var cloudStorageAccount =
            CloudStorageAccount.Parse(
            RoleEnvironment.GetConfigurationSettingValue(
"Microsoft.WindowsAzure.Plugins.Diagnostics.
 ConnectionString"));

        // Get the perf counters
config.PerformanceCounters.ScheduledTransferPeriod =
    TimeSpan.FromMinutes(1);

        // Add the perf counters
        config.PerformanceCounters.DataSources.Add(
            new PerformanceCounterConfiguration
            {
CounterSpecifier =
  @"\Processor(_Total)\% ProcessorTime",
                SampleRate = TimeSpan.FromSeconds(30)
            });
```

```
config.PerformanceCounters.DataSources.Add(
    new PerformanceCounterConfiguration
    {
        CounterSpecifier = @"\Process(aspnet_wp)\% Processor Time",
        SampleRate = TimeSpan.FromSeconds(30)
    });
config.PerformanceCounters.DataSources.Add(
    new PerformanceCounterConfiguration
    {
        CounterSpecifier = @"\Process(aspnet_wp)\Private Bytes",
        SampleRate = TimeSpan.FromSeconds(30)
    });
config.PerformanceCounters.DataSources.Add(
    new PerformanceCounterConfiguration
    {
        CounterSpecifier =
        @"\Microsoft® .NET CLR Exceptions\# Exceps thrown / sec",
        SampleRate = TimeSpan.FromSeconds(30)
    });
config.PerformanceCounters.DataSources.Add(
    new PerformanceCounterConfiguration
    {
        CounterSpecifier = @"\ASP.NET\Requests Rejected",
        SampleRate = TimeSpan.FromSeconds(30)
    });
config.PerformanceCounters.DataSources.Add(
    new PerformanceCounterConfiguration
    {
        CounterSpecifier = @"\ASP.NET\Worker Process Restarts",
        SampleRate = TimeSpan.FromSeconds(30)
    });
config.PerformanceCounters.DataSources.Add(
    new PerformanceCounterConfiguration
    {
        CounterSpecifier = @"\Memory\Available Mbytes",
        SampleRate = TimeSpan.FromSeconds(30)
    });

// Diagnostics Infrastructure logs
config.DiagnosticInfrastructureLogs.ScheduledTransferPeriod =
    System.TimeSpan.FromMinutes(1);
config.DiagnosticInfrastructureLogs.ScheduledTransferLogLevelFilter =
    LogLevel.Verbose;

// Windows Event Logs
```

```
            config.WindowsEventLog.DataSources.Add("System!*");
            config.WindowsEventLog.DataSources.Add("Application!*");
config.WindowsEventLog.ScheduledTransferPeriod =
    TimeSpan.FromMinutes(1);
config.WindowsEventLog.ScheduledTransferLogLevelFilter =
    LogLevel.Warning;

        // Azure Trace Logs
config.Logs.ScheduledTransferPeriod =
    TimeSpan.FromMinutes(1);
config.Logs.ScheduledTransferLogLevelFilter =
    LogLevel.Warning;

        // Crash Dumps
        CrashDumps.EnableCollection(true);

        // IIS Logs
config.Directories.ScheduledTransferPeriod =
    TimeSpan.FromMinutes(10);

        DiagnosticMonitor diagMonitor =
            DiagnosticMonitor.Start(cloudStorageAccount, config);

        return base.OnStart();
    }
}
```

The **Microsoft.WindowsAzure.Plugins.Diagnostics.Connection String** setting in the configuration file (.cscfg) determines the Windows Azure storage account to use for the performance counter data.

This must be the same storage account that Tailspin configures for the **dataPointsStoreAccount** setting in the Autoscaling Application Block configuration.

IMPLEMENTING THROTTLING BEHAVIOR

Tailspin uses reactive rules to scale and throttle the Tailspin Surveys application. To implement the throttling behavior, Tailspin modified the Surveys application to change its behavior when a reactive rule changes the throttling mode. The following code snippet shows example reactive rules that request throttling actions in the Surveys application. These two example rules assign values to the configuration setting **ThrottlingMode** in Windows Azure roles.

```XML
<rule name="TenantWeb &amp; Survey Worker - Burst - Throttle"
          description="..."
          enabled="true">
    <actions>
<changeSetting target="SurveyWorkers"
        settingName="ThrottlingMode"
            value="ReduceSystemLoad" />
<changeSetting target="TenantWebSite"
        settingName="ThrottlingMode"
            value="ReduceSystemLoad" />
    </actions>
    <when>
      ...
    </when>
    <rank>0</rank>
  </rule>
<rule name="TenantWeb &amp; Survey Worker - Burst – Stop
          throttling"
        description="..."
        enabled="true">
    <actions>
<changeSetting target="TenantWebSite"
        settingName="ThrottlingMode"
            value="Normal" />
<changeSetting target="SurveyWorkers"
        settingName="ThrottlingMode"
            value="Normal" />
    </actions>
    <when>
      ...
    </when>
    <rank>0</rank>
  </rule>
```

These settings must exist in the target role service definitions. The following snippet shows this in the **Tailspin.Surveys.Cloud** service definition file (*.csdef).

```xml
XML
<WorkerRole name="Tailspin.Workers.Surveys">
    <ConfigurationSettings>
      ...
      <Setting name="ThrottlingMode" />
    </ConfigurationSettings>
    ...
  </WorkerRole>
```

The Surveys application uses the throttling mode value to change the behavior of the application. For example, in the Tailspin Surveys worker role the **QueueHandler** and **BatchProcessingQueueHandler** classes check the value of the setting before processing any messages. The following code sample shows how the **TransferSurveysToSql AzureCommand** class checks the configuration setting.

```csharp
C#
public bool CanRun
{
    get
    {
      return
      !this.configurationSettings.ConfigurationSettingEquals(
      AzureConstants.ConfigurationSettings.ThrottlingMode,
      "ReduceSystemLoad");
    }
}
```

The Tailspin tenant web role also uses the setting to inform users when the application is being throttled. The Index.aspx file in the **Tailspin.Web.Areas.Survey.Views.Surveys** folder reads the configuration value, and the view then displays a message when the throttling mode is set to **ReduceSystemLoad**.

EDITING AND SAVING RULES

This section describes how Tailspin built its web hosted autoscaling rule editor so that it saves the rules to the correct location, ensures that the rule definitions for the Surveys application comply with the Autoscaling Application Block rules schema, and handles cross-validation with the Surveys application's service information definition.

Discovering the Location of the Rules Store

To be able to load and save Tailspin Survey's autoscaling rules to the correct location, the application must read the Autoscaling Application Block configuration from the web.config file of the web role that hosts the application block. The following code sample from the **SharedContainerBootstrapper** class in the **Tailspin.Shared** project shows how this is done.

```csharp
C#
private static IConfigurationFileAccess
CreateServiceInformationModelConfigurationFileAccess
  (IUnityContainer container)
{
    AutoscalingSettings settings =
        (AutoscalingSettings)ConfigurationManager
        .GetSection("autoscalingConfiguration");

BlobServiceInformationStoreData serviceInformationStoreData =
    (BlobServiceInformationStoreData)settings
        .ServiceInformationStores
        .Get(settings.ServiceInformationStoreName);

return new BlobConfigurationFileAccess(
    new AzureStorageAccount(serviceInformationStoreData.
                            StorageAccount),
        serviceInformationStoreData.BlobContainerName,
        serviceInformationStoreData.BlobName,
        serviceInformationStoreData.MonitoringRate,
        container.Resolve<ILogger>());
}
```

Reading and Writing to the Rules Store

The Autoscaling Application Block includes the **RuleSetSerializer** class that uses instances of the **RuleSetElement** class to deserialize from and serialize to the rules store. The **LoadRuleSet** and **Save CurrentRuleSet** methods in the **RuleSetModelStore** class in the **AutoScaling/Rules** folder in the **Tailspin.Shared** project illustrate how the Surveys application uses the **RuleSetSerializer** class.

```
C#
using
  Microsoft.Practices.EnterpriseLibrary.WindowsAzure.Autoscaling.
  Rules.Configuration;
...
private readonly IConfigurationFileAccess fileAccess;
private readonly RuleSetModelToXmlElementConverter
              ruleSetModelToXmlElementConverter;
...
private RuleSetModel currentRuleSet;
private RuleSetSerializer serializer;
public RuleSetModelStore(
    RuleSetModelToXmlElementConverter
    ruleSetModelToXmlElementConverter,
    [Dependency("RuleSetModel")] IConfigurationFileAccess
    fileAccess,
    RetryManager retryManager)
{
...
this.ruleSetModelToXmlElementConverter =
    ruleSetModelToXmlElementConverter;
this.fileAccess = fileAccess;

    this.CreateSerializer();

    this.LoadRuleSet();
}

private void CreateSerializer()
{
    var allExtensions = new IRuleSerializationExtension[]
      {
        new AssemblyRuleSerializationExtension(
          typeof(ActiveSurveysOperandElement).Assembly.FullName)
      };

    this.serializer = new RuleSetSerializer(
allExtensions.SelectMany(e => e.CustomActionDefinitions),
allExtensions.SelectMany(e =>
                    e.CustomParameterDefinitions));
}

private void LoadRuleSet()
{
    string fileContent = this.GetFileContent();
```

```
    RuleSetElement ruleSetElement;
    if (string.IsNullOrEmpty(fileContent))
    {
        ruleSetElement = new RuleSetElement();
    }
    else
    {
    ruleSetElement = this.serializer.Deserialize(new
                    StringReader(fileContent));
    }

    this.currentRuleSet = this.ruleSetModelToXmlElementConverter
      .ConvertElementToModel(ruleSetElement);
}

...
public void SaveCurrentRuleSet()
{
    lock (this.syncRoot)
    {
        var writer = new StringWriter();
        RuleSetElement element =
            this.ruleSetModelToXmlElementConverter
            .ConvertModelToElement(this.currentRuleSet);
        this.serializer.Serialize(writer, element);
        this.SetFileContent(writer.ToString());
    }
}
```

Creating Valid Autoscaling Rules

Tailspin uses the classes in the **Microsoft.Practices.Enterprise
Library.WindowsAzure.Autoscaling.Rules.Configuration**
namespace in the Autoscaling Application Block to ensure that the
Surveys application rule editor creates autoscaling rules that are valid
according the autoscaling rules schema. For example, the **Constraint
RuleToXmlElementConverter** class converts between the **Constraint
RuleModel** class used by the Tailspin Surveys rule editor, and the
ConstraintRuleElement class that the Autoscaling Application Block
uses. For additional examples, see the other converter classes in the
Tailspin.Shared.AutoScaling.Rules.XmlElementConverters
namespace.

It is easier to bind the
Tailspin model classes
to the UI than to bind
the Autoscaling
Application Block
element classes to
the UI.

Validating Target Names in the Rule Definitions

Target names in rule actions are aliases for roles and scale groups. The source name of some operands in the rule definitions is also an alias for a role. These aliases are defined in the service information definition for your application. In the rule editor in Tailspin Surveys, the text box where the user enters the target name supports auto-completion based on a list of role aliases and scale group names from the service information definition. The following code sample from the _ConstraintRuleActionEditor.cshtml file in the **Tailspin.Web.Management** project shows how the UI element is constructed.

CSHTML
```
<tr>
  <td>@Html.HiddenFor(m => m.Id)@Html.EditorFor(m => m.Target,
  "_AutoComplete", new { @class = "targetTextBox",
  url = @Url.Action("GetTargets", "Home",
  new { Area = "ServiceInformation" }),
  placeholder =
  "{Target Name}" })@Html.ValidationMessageFor(m => m.Target)
  </td>
...
</tr>
```

The following code sample from the **HomeController** class in the **Tailspin.Web.Management.Areas.ServiceInformation.Controllers** namespace shows the **GetTargets** method that is invoked from the view above.

C#
```
public ActionResult GetTargets()
{
    var roleAliasses =
        this.serviceInformationModelStore.GetAllRoles()
            .Select(r => r.Alias);
    var scaleGroups =
        this.serviceInformationModelStore
            .GetScaleGroups().Select(r => r.Alias);

    return this.Json(roleAliasses.Union(scaleGroups).Where
        (s => !string.IsNullOrEmpty(s)),
            JsonRequestBehavior.AllowGet);
}
```

EDITING AND SAVING THE SERVICE INFORMATION

The implementation of the service information authoring features described in this section is very similar to the implementation of the rule editing and saving features in Tailspin Surveys.

The **ServiceInformationModelStore** class is responsible for discovering the location of the service information store by querying the application block's configuration file and is also responsible for enabling the Surveys application to be able to read and write the service information. The application block does not include a custom XML serializer class for the service information, so the **ServiceInformation ModelStore** class uses an **XMLSerializer** instance to handle the deserialization and serialization to XML.

The service information model classes in the **Tailspin.Shared. AutoScaling.ServiceInformation** namespace provide their own conversion to the element classes in the Autoscaling Application Block **Microsoft.Practices.EnterpriseLibrary.WindowsAzure.Autoscaling. ServiceModel.Configuration** namespace. Tailspin uses the element classes in the block to ensure that the Surveys application creates a valid service information XML document to save to the service information store.

VISUALIZING THE AUTOSCALING ACTIONS

The operators at Tailspin want to be able to see the autoscaling operations that have occurred in the Surveys application in order to help them understand how the Autoscaling Application Block is working. Tailspin has developed a number of visualization charts that plot the number of role instances and show the maximum and minimum constraint values over time.

To create these charts, Tailspin needs information about the current and recent number of role instances for all of the roles that the block is managing as well as information about the maximum and minimum constraint values that were in effect for the period shown on the chart so that these can also be shown on the charts.

The Autoscaling Application Block records the number of role instances for each of the Windows Azure roles that it is managing as data points in the data points store. This store is a table in Windows Azure storage.

Whenever the block evaluates its autoscaling rules, it writes a log message that includes details of the maximum and minimum instance counts that were permitted at the time the rules were evaluated and details of the scaling action, if any, which were suggested by the reactive rules.

The following code sample from the **GraphController** class in the **Tailspin.Web.Management.Areas.Monitoring.Controllers** namespace shows how the management website retrieves the instance count values from the data points store to plot on a chart.

```csharp
private void AddInstanceCountSeries(Chart chart,
                        DateTimeFilter dateTimeFilter,
                        string sourceName, string sourceAlias)
{
    IEnumerable<DataPoint> dataPoints = this.dataPointsStore.Get(
        sourceAlias,
        "RoleInstanceCount",
        "RoleInstanceCount",
        dateTimeFilter.GetEffectiveStartDate(),
        dateTimeFilter.GetEffectiveEndDate());

    Series series = chart.Series.Add(sourceName);
    series.ChartType = SeriesChartType.StepLine;
    series.ToolTip =
        "TimeStamp = #VALX{d} \n Number of instances = #VALY{d}";
    series.ChartArea = ChartArea;
    series.BorderWidth = 5;
    series.Color = this.GetRoleColor(sourceAlias);

    foreach (DataPoint dp in dataPoints)
    {
        series.Points.AddXY(dp.DataTimestamp.DateTime.
            ToLocalTime(), dp.Value);
    }

    if (!dataPoints.Any())
    {
        series.Name += " (No matching datapoints found)";
    }

    AddEmptyStartEndPoints(series, dateTimeFilter);
    this.RememberMaximum(chart,
                        dataPoints.MaxOrZero(m => m.Value));
}
```

In this example, the **sourceName** string is the name of the role, and Tailspin uses a **DateTimeFilter** object to specify the range of data points to retrieve. The **Get** method is provided by the **AzureStorage DataPointStore** class in the Autoscaling Application Block.

The following code sample from the **GraphController** class in the **Tailspin.Web.Management.Areas.Monitoring.Controllers** namespace shows how the management website retrieves the maximum and minimum permitted instance count values from the data points store to plot on a chart.

C#
```csharp
private void AddMinMaxSeries(Chart chart, DateTimeFilter
    dateTimeFilter, string sourceName, string sourceAlias)
{
    IEnumerable<WADLogsTableEntity> minMaxLogMessages =
        this.logDataStore.Get(
            dateTimeFilter.GetEffectiveStartDate(),
            dateTimeFilter.GetEffectiveEndDate(),
        Constants.Scaling.Events.RequestForConfigurationChange);

    List<MinMaxInstanceCountDataPoint> minMaxLogMessagesForRole =
        minMaxLogMessages.SelectMany(
            l => this.CreateMinMaxModels(l, sourceAlias)).ToList();

    Series minSeries = chart.Series.Add(string.Empty);
    minSeries.ChartArea = ChartArea;
    minSeries.ChartType = SeriesChartType.StackedArea;
    minSeries.IsVisibleInLegend = false;
    minSeries.Color = Color.Transparent;

    foreach (MinMaxInstanceCountDataPoint minMaxLogMessage in
        minMaxLogMessagesForRole)
    {
        minSeries.Points.AddXY(
            minMaxLogMessage.EventDateTime.ToLocalTime(),
            minMaxLogMessage.MinInstanceCount);
    }

    Series maxSeries = chart.Series.Add("Minimum and Maximum
        instance count");
    maxSeries.ChartArea = ChartArea;
    maxSeries.ChartType = SeriesChartType.StackedArea;
    maxSeries.Color = Color.FromArgb(98, 0, 73, 255);
                    // Transparent blue

    foreach (MinMaxInstanceCountDataPoint minMaxLogMessage in
        minMaxLogMessagesForRole)
    {
        var index = maxSeries.Points.AddXY(
```

```
        var index = maxSeries.Points.AddXY(
          minMaxLogMessage.EventDateTime.ToLocalTime(),
          minMaxLogMessage.MaxInstanceCount -
          minMaxLogMessage.MinInstanceCount);
        maxSeries.Points[index].ToolTip = string.Format(
          "Min Instance Count = {0}\nMax Instance Count = {1}",
            minMaxLogMessage.MinInstanceCount,
            +minMaxLogMessage.MaxInstanceCount);
    }

    if (!minMaxLogMessagesForRole.Any())
    {
        minSeries.Name += " (No matching datapoints found)";
        maxSeries.Name += " (No matching datapoints found)";
    }

    this.RememberMaximum(chart,
                    minMaxLogMessagesForRole.MaxOrZero(m =>
                                m.MaxInstanceCount));
}
```

If you regularly purge old log data from the Windows Azure diagnostics log tables, this will limit how far back you can view this data on the chart.

In this example, the **sourceName** string is again the name of the role, and Tailspin again uses a **DateTimeFilter** object to specify the range of data points to retrieve. In this example, Tailspin implemented the **Get** method in the **AzureStorageWadLogDataStore** class in the **Tailspin.Web.Management.Areas.Monitoring.Models** namespace.

To plot the charts, Tailspin used the ASP.NET charting controls to enable clickable behavior. Users can click on the charts to discover more detail about the data behind the points.

If you want to learn more about the way that the Tailspin Surveys application renders the charts, take a look at the classes in the **Tailspin.Web.Management.Areas.Monitoring** namespace.

IMPLEMENTING A CUSTOM ACTION

This section describes how Tailspin implemented a custom action that it can use alongside existing scaling actions to notify operators by an SMS message when important scaling operations are taking place. The Autoscaling Application Block provides an extension point for creating custom actions. Tailspin must also ensure that its rule editing UI can load and save the custom action definitions to the rules store.

Integrating a Custom Action with the Autoscaling Application Block

Actions are a part of reactive autoscaling rules that the application block reads from its rules store. Tailspin uses the default blob XML rules store, so Tailspin must provide a way for the application block to deserialize its custom action from the XML document.

The following snippet shows how Tailspin might add a custom action in the rules store.

Tailspin is currently not using this custom action.

For Tailspin, adding a custom action requires two sets of related changes. The first is to ensure that the Autoscaling Application Block knows about the custom action, the second is to ensure that the rule editing UI knows about the custom action.

If Tailspin operators edited rules in an XML editor, Tailspin could add validation and IntelliSense® behavior to the editor if it created an XML schema for the *http://Tailspin/SendSMS* namespace.

```XML
<reactiveRules>
  <rule ...>
    ...
    <actions>
      <smsAction xmlns="http://Tailspin/SendSMS"
          phoneNumber="+8888" message="Alert, reactive rule..."/>
    </actions>
  </rule>
</reactiveRules>
```

Tailspin first created the class shown in the following code sample to perform the deserialization of the custom action from the XML rules store. Notice how the attributes are used to identify the XML element, attributes, and namespace.

```C#
[XmlRoot(ElementName = "smsAction",
        Namespace = "http://Tailspin/SendSMS")]
public class SendSmsActionElement : ReactiveRuleActionElement
{
    [XmlAttribute("phoneNumber")]
    public string PhoneNumber { get; set; }

    [XmlAttribute("message")]
    public string Message { get; set; }
```

```csharp
    public override ReactiveRuleAction CreateAction()
    {
        return new SendSmsAction
            {
                Message = this.Message,
                PhoneNumber = this.PhoneNumber
            };
    }
}
```

The **CreateAction** method returns a **SendSmsAction** instance that performs the custom action. The following code snippet shows the **SendSmsAction** class, which extends the **ReactiveRuleAction** class.

C#
```csharp
public class SendSmsAction : ReactiveRuleAction
{

    public SendSmsAction()
    {
    }

    public string PhoneNumber { get; set; }

    public string Message { get; set; }

    public override IEnumerable<RuleEvaluationResult> GetResults(
        ReactiveRule forRule, IRuleEvaluationContext context)
    {
        return new[]
            {
                new SendSmsActionResult(forRule)
                    {
                        Message = this.Message,
                        PhoneNumber = this.PhoneNumber
                    }
            };
    }
}
```

The rules evaluator in the block calls the **GetResults** method of all the actions for the current rule, and then calls the **Execute** method on each **RuleEvaluationResult** object that is returned. The following code snippet shows the **SendSmsActionResult** class (the **Execute ActionResult** class extends the **RuleEvaluationResult** class).

C#
```csharp
public class SendSmsActionResult : ExecuteActionResult
{
    private readonly ISmsSender smsSender;

    public SendSmsActionResult(Rule sourceRule)
        : base(sourceRule)
    {
        this.smsSender =
    EnterpriseLibraryContainer.Current.GetInstance<ISmsSender>();
    }

    public string PhoneNumber { get; set; }

    public string Message { get; set; }

    public override string Description
    {
        get
        {
            return string.Format("Sends an SMS to number: '{0}'
            with message: '{1}'", this.PhoneNumber, this.Message);
        }
    }

    public override void Execute(IRuleEvaluationContext context)
    {
        this.smsSender.Send(this.PhoneNumber, this.Message);
    }
}
```

The block uses the **Description** property when it logs the sending of the SMS message.

Finally, Tailspin used the Enterprise Library configuration tool to tell the Autoscaling Application Block about the custom action.

If you throw an exception in the **Execute** method it must be of type **ActionExecution Exception**.

XML
```xml
<autoscalingConfiguration ... >
    ...
    <rulesStores>
        <add name="Blob Rules Store" type=... >
            <extensionAssemblies>
                <add name="Tailspin.Shared" />
            </extensionAssemblies>
        </add>
```

The example loads the assembly containing the custom **ActiveSurveysOperandElement** class. This assembly also contains the custom **SendSmsActionElement** class. The extension is loaded explicitly in code, because the management website is not hosting the Autoscaling Application Block and so cannot use the configuration setting to load it.

```
    </rulesStores>
    ...
</autoscalingConfiguration>
```

The **extensionAssemblies** element adds the name of the assembly that contains the classes that define the custom action.

Integrating a Custom Action with the Tailspin Surveys Rule Editor

The Tailspin Surveys rule editor allows administrators to edit the autoscaling rules for the Surveys application in a web UI. This editor can read and save rule definitions to the rules store that the Autoscaling Application Block uses. The block treats the rules store as a read-only store, but the block includes a **RuleSetSerializer** class, which provides support for saving rule definitions to the store.

Tailspin configures the **RuleSetSerializer** instance that the rule editor uses with the details of the custom action and operand. The following code snippet from the **RuleSetModelStore** class shows how the two extensions (the custom action and operand) are loaded.

```csharp
private RuleSetSerializer serializer;

public RuleSetModelStore(RuleSetModelToXmlElementConverter
        ruleSetModelToXmlElementConverter,
        [Dependency("RuleSetModel")] IConfigurationFileAccess
        fileAccess, RetryManager retryManager)
{
    ...
    this.CreateSerializer();
    ...
}


private void CreateSerializer()
{
    var allExtensions = new IRuleSerializationExtension[]
        {
            new AssemblyRuleSerializationExtension(
            typeof(ActiveSurveysOperandElement).Assembly.FullName)
        };
    this.serializer = new RuleSetSerializer(
        allExtensions.SelectMany(e => e.CustomActionDefinitions),
    allExtensions.SelectMany(e => e.CustomParameterDefinitions));
}
```

After the extensions are added to the serializer, the rules editor can load and save rules that include the custom actions and operands that Tailspin has created.

You do not need to load the assembly that contains your extensions programmatically in the project that hosts the Autoscaling Application Block because the application block already contains code that will load extension assemblies based on the entries in the **autoscalingConfiguration** section of the configuration file. In the Tailspin Surveys solution, the **Tailspin.Workers.Autoscaling** worker role hosts the Autoscaling Application Block and thus loads the extensions automatically; however, the **Tailspin.Web.Management** web role (which does not host the Autoscaling Application Block) must load the extensions programmatically.

IMPLEMENTING CUSTOM OPERANDS

The process for creating a custom operand is very similar to the process for creating a custom action. Tailspin implemented two custom operands that enable the rules to use the number of active surveys and the current number of tenants as metrics in a reactive rule.

The Autoscaling Application Block provides an extension point for creating custom operands. Tailspin must also ensure that its rule editing UI can load and save the custom operands to the rules store.

For a custom action, you must extend the **Reactive RuleAction** and **Execute ActionResult** classes; for a custom operand, you must provide an implementation of the **IDataPoints Collector** interface.

Integrating a Custom Operand with the Autoscaling Application Block

Operands are a part of reactive autoscaling rules that the application block reads from its rules store. Tailspin uses the default blob XML rules store, so Tailspin must provide a way for the application block to deserialize its custom operand from the XML document.

The following snippet shows an example of Tailspin's **active SurveysOperand** custom operand in the rules store.

```XML
<operands>
    ...
    <activeSurveysOperand
     alias="Tailspin_ActiveSurveyCount_Avg_10m"
     timespan="00:10:00"
     aggregate="Average"
     minNumberOfAnswers="0"
     xmlns="http://Tailspin/ActiveSurveys" />
    ...
</operands>
```

Tailspin first created the class shown in the following code sample to perform the deserialization of the **activeSurveysOperand** custom operand from the XML rules store. Notice how the attributes are used to identify the XML element, attributes, and namespace.

```csharp
[XmlRoot(ElementName = "activeSurveysOperand",
         Namespace = "http://Tailspin/ActiveSurveys")]
public class ActiveSurveysOperandElement :
                  DataPointsParameterElement
{

    [XmlAttribute("minNumberOfAnswers")]
    public int MinNumberOfAnswers( get; set; }

    protected override string DataPointName
    {
        get
        {
            return this.DataPointType;
        }
    }

    protected override string DataPointType
    {
        get
        {
            return "Number of Active Surveys";
        }
    }

    protected override string SourceName
    {
        get
        {
            return "Tailspin";
        }
    }
}
```

If Tailspin operators edited rules in an XML editor, Tailspin could add validation and IntelliSense behavior to the editor if it created XML schemas for the *http://Tailspin/ ActiveSurveys* and *http://Tailspin/ TenantCount* namespaces.

```
protected override Func<IServiceInformationStore,
    IEnumerable<IDataPointsCollector>> GetCollectorsFactory()
{
    var samplingRate = ActiveSurveysDataPointsCollector
                    .DefaultPerformanceCounterSamplingRate;
    return (sis) =>
        new[]
        {
            new ActiveSurveysDataPointsCollector(
                EnterpriseLibraryContainer.Current
                  .GetInstance<ISurveyStore>(),
                EnterpriseLibraryContainer.Current
                  .GetInstance<ISurveyAnswersSummaryStore>(),
                samplingRate,
                this.MinNumberOfAnswers,
                this.SourceName,
                this.DataPointType,
                this.DataPointName)
        };


    }
}
```

The **MinNumberOfAnswers** property defines an optional attribute that Tailspin uses to filter the list of surveys that it is counting. For example, if Tailspin sets the **minNumberOfAnswers** attribute of the operand to 5000, then the **activeSurveysOperand** will only count surveys that currently have at least 5000 answers collected.

The **GetCollectorsFactory** method instantiates an **Active SurveysDataPointsCollector** object that performs the custom data collection operation. The following code snippet shows the **Active SurveysDataPointsCollector** class, which implements the **IData PointsCollector** interface. This class is responsible for collecting the data points. The **Collect** method uses the **FilterSurveys** method to retrieve only surveys that have at least the minimum number of answers specified by the **minNumberOfAnswers** attribute in the rules store.

```csharp
C#
public class ActiveSurveysDataPointsCollector : IDataPointsCollector
{

    private readonly ISurveyStore surveyStore;

    private readonly ISurveyAnswersSummaryStore surveyAnswersSummaryStore;

    private readonly TimeSpan samplingRate;

    private readonly int minimumNumberOfAnswers;

    private readonly string sourceName;

    private readonly string dataPointType;

    private readonly string dataPointName;

    public ActiveSurveysDataPointsCollector(ISurveyStore surveyStore,
      ISurveyAnswersSummaryStore surveyAnswersSummaryStore,
      TimeSpan samplingRate, int minNumberOfAnswers, string sourceName, string
      dataPointType, string dataPointName)
    {
        this.surveyStore = surveyStore;
        this.surveyAnswersSummaryStore = surveyAnswersSummaryStore;
        this.samplingRate = samplingRate;
        this.minimumNumberOfAnswers = minNumberOfAnswers;
        this.sourceName = sourceName;
        this.dataPointType = dataPointType;
        this.dataPointName = dataPointName;
    }

    public static TimeSpan DefaultPerformanceCounterSamplingRate
    {
        get { return TimeSpan.FromMinutes(2); }
    }

    public TimeSpan SamplingRate
    {
        get { return this.samplingRate; }
    }

    public string Key
    {
        get { return string.Format(CultureInfo.InvariantCulture,
          "{0}|{1}", this.minimumNumberOfAnswers, this.samplingRate); }
```

```csharp
    }

    public IEnumerable<DataPoint> Collect(DateTimeOffset collectionTime)
    {
        IEnumerable<Survey> surveys;
        try
        {
            surveys = this.surveyStore.GetActiveSurveys(FilterSurveys).ToList();
        }
        catch (StorageClientException ex)
        {
            throw new DataPointsCollectionException(
              "Could not retrieve surveys", ex);
        }

        return new[]
            {
                new DataPoint
                {
                    CreationTime = collectionTime,
                    Source = this.sourceName,
                    Type = this.dataPointType,
                    Name = this.dataPointName,
                    Value = surveys.Count(),
                    DataTimestamp = collectionTime
                }
            };
    }

    private bool FilterSurveys(string tenantname, string slugname)
    {
        if (this.minimumNumberOfAnswers == 0)
        {
            return true;
        }
        var answersSummary =
          this.surveyAnswersSummaryStore.GetSurveyAnswersSummary(
          tenantname, slugname);
        if (answersSummary == null)
        {
            return false;
        }
        return answersSummary.TotalAnswers > this.minimumNumberOfAnswers;
    }
}
```

Finally, Tailspin used the Enterprise Library configuration tool to tell the Autoscaling Application Block about the custom action. Because the custom operand and custom action are in the same assembly, there is only a single entry in the **extensionAssemblies** element.

```XML
<autoscalingConfiguration ... >
    ...
    <rulesStores>
        <add name="Blob Rules Store" type=... >
            <extensionAssemblies>
                <add name="Tailspin.Shared" />
            </extensionAssemblies>
        </add>
    </rulesStores>
    ...
</autoscalingConfiguration>
```

Integrating a Custom Operand with the Tailspin Surveys Rule Editor

This is done in exactly the same way as integrating the custom action with the rules editor. Because the custom operand and custom action are in the same assembly, the **CreateSerializer** method in the **Rule SetModelStore** class only adds a single extension assembly.

Configuring Logging in Tailspin Surveys

The Autoscaling Application Block allows you to choose between logging implementations. Because the Autoscaling Application Block is hosted in a Windows Azure worker role and Tailspin does not require any of the additional features offered by the Enterprise Library Logging Application Block, Tailspin uses the logging infrastructure defined in the **System.Diagnostics** namespace. The following snippet from the configuration for the Windows Azure worker role that hosts the Autoscaling Application Block shows the logging configuration for Tailspin Surveys. The **autoscalingConfiguration** section selects the system diagnostics logging infrastructure for the Autoscaling Application Block, and the **system.diagnostics** section configures the logging sources for the log messages from the block.

```XML
<autoscalingConfiguration loggerName="Source Logger" ...>
    <loggers>
        <add name="Source Logger" type="Microsoft.Practices.EnterpriseLibrary
            .WindowsAzure.Autoscaling.Logging.SystemDiagnosticsLogger,
            Microsoft.Practices.EnterpriseLibrary.WindowsAzure.Autoscaling />
    </loggers>
    ...
</autoscalingConfiguration>
...
<system.diagnostics>
  <sources>
    <source name="Autoscaling General" switchValue="All">
      <listeners>
        <add name="AzureDiag" />
        <remove name="Default"  />
      </listeners>
    </source>
    <source name="Autoscaling Updates" switchValue="All">
      <listeners>
        <add name="AzureDiag" />
        <remove name="Default"  />
      </listeners>
    </source>
  </sources>
  <sharedListeners>
    <add type="Microsoft.WindowsAzure.Diagnostics.DiagnosticMonitorTraceListener,
        Microsoft.WindowsAzure.Diagnostics, Version=1.0.0.0, Culture=neutral,
        PublicKeyToken=31bf3856ad364e35"
        name="AzureDiag"/>
  </sharedListeners>
  <trace>
    <listeners>
      <add type="Microsoft.WindowsAzure.Diagnostics.DiagnosticMonitorTraceListener,
          Microsoft.WindowsAzure.Diagnostics, Version=1.0.0.0, Culture=neutral,
          PublicKeyToken=31bf3856ad364e35"
          name="AzureDiagnostics">
        <filter type="" />
      </add>
    </listeners>
  </trace>
</system.diagnostics>
```

*The values of the **type** attributes are shown split over multiple lines. The configuration file should not contain any line breaks.*

Setup and Physical Deployment

This section discusses considerations you should take into account when deploying the Tailspin Surveys application.

CERTIFICATES AND TAILSPIN SURVEYS DEPLOYMENT

When you deploy the Tailspin Surveys application you must also deploy a number of certificates. This section describes the role of the certificates, where they are deployed, and how to obtain or generate suitable certificates. This section focuses on the certificates used directly by Tailspin Surveys and the Autoscaling Application Block. For more information about the certificates used by the simulated issuers that handle claims-based identity management, see the guide *"Developing Applications for the Cloud"* on MSDN.

When you deploy the Tailspin Surveys application, there are two certificates that you must deploy. One certificate enables Tailspin Surveys to use an HTTPS endpoint, and the other certificate is used by the Autoscaling Application Block to make Windows Azure Service Management API calls to the Tailspin Surveys hosted service. The block uses these API calls to collect data from Tailspin Surveys and to make scaling requests.

Deploying a Service Certificate to Enable SSL

The Dependency Checker tool that you use to install the Tailspin Surveys solution on your local development machine includes a sample **localhost** certificate that you can use to enable HTTPS when you deploy the Surveys application to Windows Azure. Both the Tailspin Surveys tenant website and management website use HTTPS endpoints. The following snippet from the service definition file (.csdef) for the **Tailspin.Web** role shows the certificate and endpoint definitions.

```XML
<WebRole name="Tailspin.Web" ...>

  ...

   <Certificates>
     <Certificate name="localhost_ssl"
                  storeLocation="LocalMachine"
                  storeName="My" />
   </Certificates>
   <Endpoints>
    <InputEndpoint name="HttpsIn" protocol="https" port="443"
     certificate="localhost_ssl" />
   </Endpoints>

   ...

</WebRole>
```

The service configuration file identifies the certificate to use by its thumbprint.

> The **localhost** *certificate included with the Tailspin Surveys solution is for demonstration purposes only and should not be used in a production environment.*

You must upload the service certificate you plan to use to secure your HTTPS endpoints to the certificate store in your Windows Azure portal and to ensure that the thumbprint of the certificate that you upload matches the thumbprint in the service configuration file (.cscfg).

For more information about obtaining an SSL certificate, see *"How to Obtain an SSL Certificate."*

For more information about configuring HTTPS endpoints in Windows Azure web roles, see *"How to Configure an SSL Certificate on an HTTPS Endpoint."*

Deploying the Management Certificate to Enable Scaling Operations

In the Tailspin Surveys application, the Autoscaling Application Block is hosted in a separate worker role from the main Surveys application. The Autoscaling Application Block uses the Windows Azure Service Management API to perform scaling actions on the Tailspin Surveys roles, and this API is secured using a management certificate. This section describes how Tailspin created and deployed this management certificate.

Tailspin uses a standard X.509 v3 certificate with a key length of 2048 bits for the management certificate. To generate this self-signed certificate, Tailspin ran the following command in the Visual Studio command prompt window to create the certificate and install it in the local certificate store.

```
makecert -r -pe -n "CN= Tailspin Management Certificate" -b
05/10/2010 -e 12/22/2012  -ss my -sr localmachine -sky exchange
-sp "Microsoft RSA SChannel Cryptographic Provider" -sy 12
```

Tailspin then uploaded the public key to the **Management Certificates** folder in the Windows Azure subscription that hosts the Tailspin Surveys application, and the private key to the **Service Certificates** folder in the hosted service that hosts the Autoscaling Application Block. This enables the Autoscaling Application Block to secure the Windows Azure Service Management API calls that it makes to the subscription that hosts the Tailspin Surveys application.

For more information on management and service certificates in Windows Azure, see *"Managing Certificates in Windows Azure."*

You can use the Certificates snap-in in the Microsoft Management Console (MMC) to export a file that contains the public key (.cer) and a file that contains the private key (.pfx).

Deploying Tailspin Surveys in Multiple Geographic Locations

The sample version of the Tailspin Surveys application is designed to deploy to a single data center where the Autoscaling Application Block can scale the application in and out by adding and removing role instances. This represents the first phase of Tailspin's plan to roll out autoscaling to all the locations where the Tailspin Surveys application is currently deployed; these locations are the North Central US Data Center, the West Europe Data Center, and the Southeast Asia Data Center. Tailspin wants to be able to manage the autoscaling behavior in all the data centers from a single, centralized management application.

Figure 2 shows the current architecture in the sample solution in which Tailspin uses the Autoscaling Application Block to manage the Surveys application in a single data center.

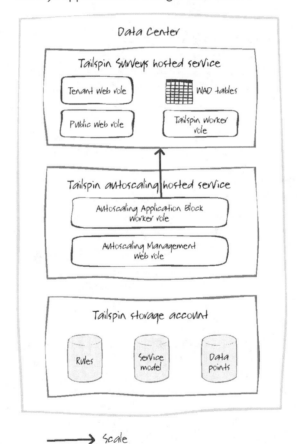

FIGURE 2
Tailspin Surveys deployed to a single data center

Although Tailspin could use the same architecture in the other data centers, this would mean that each data center has its own management website. Tailspin wants to use a single management website to gain a consolidated view of the complete autoscaling infrastructure of the Tailspin Surveys application.

Tailspin considered two alternative architectures for its autoscaling infrastructure. Figure 3 shows the first alternative where the Autoscaling Application Block and management web application are hosted in the US data center.

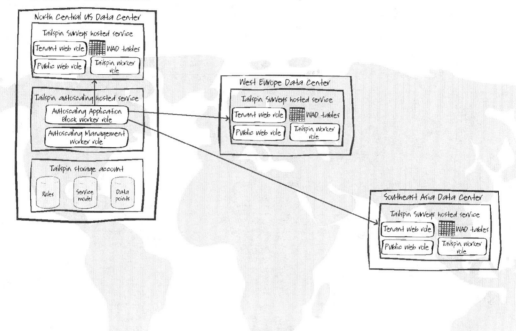

FIGURE 3
Option 1: deploying the Autoscaling Application Block centrally

Figure 4 shows the second alternative, in which the Autoscaling Application Block is deployed in each data center and the management web application is still deployed in the US data center.

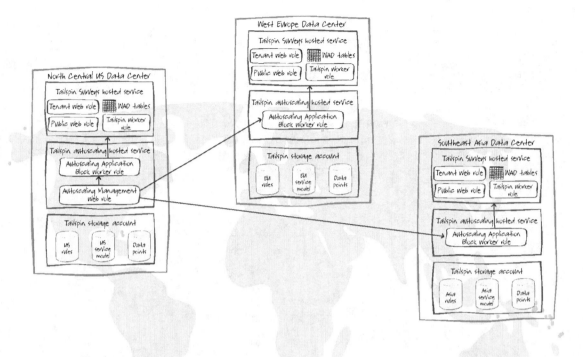

FIGURE 4
Option 2: deploying the Autoscaling Application Block in each data center

Both of these alternatives achieve Tailspin's goal of managing the autoscaling infrastructure from a central management application, but there are a number of trade-offs to consider between the two alternatives. Some of these trade-offs are summarized below.

Data Transfer Costs

Although both alternatives will involve data transfers from the remote data centers to the US data center, in option 1, all of the performance counter metrics that the application block collects from the Windows Azure diagnostics tables is transferred to the US data center and stored in the data points store. In option 2, all of the performance counter data is stored in a local data points store. However, any metric data that the management application uses for displaying charts and reports still has to be brought over the network.

Tailspin anticipates that the data transfer costs will be lower if it adopts option 2. Option 2 will also reduce the time taken to transfer data to the data points store and minimize the risk of any transient network conditions impacting on the autoscaling process.

Role Instances

Both alternatives need only a single role instance for the management application. Tailspin does not anticipate heavy usage of this application, so it can use a small instance.

In option 1, there is a single instance of the worker role that hosts the Autoscaling Application Block running in the US data center. Tailspin estimates that it can use either a small or medium-sized role instance in this scenario.

In option 2, there is a single instance of the worker role that hosts the Autoscaling Application Block running in each data center. Tailspin estimates that it can use a small role instance for this worker role in each data center.

Option 2 will use more role instances than option 1.

> You can use Windows Azure storage analytics to gain deeper insight into your data usage. For more information, see "Storage Analytics Overview."

Configuration Differences

Option 1 stores all the service information and autoscaling rules in stores in the US data center. If Tailspin is to use different rules in each data center it must be careful to adopt naming conventions to refer to the roles in the different data centers, and the rules and operands that apply to those roles. With option 2, each data center has its own rules store and service information.

In both cases, it is possible to use different rules in each data center if the autoscaling requirements differ. With option 1, Tailspin must take more care to make the rules manageable by adopting suitable naming conventions.

Application Differences

The existing management web application will work unchanged with option 1 as it is designed to work with a single service information store and a single rules store. It would not be too difficult for Tailspin to enhance the management website to work with multiple information stores and rules stores as required by option 2.

> Tailspin plans to use only single instances of the autoscaling roles because it does not require the Windows Azure SLA guarantees for these roles.

The existing custom operands will not work with option 1 because they are not designed to work with multiple instances of the Tailspin Surveys application; there is currently no way to configure them to collect data from a specific instance of the Surveys application. The custom operands will work unchanged with option 2 because each instance of the Autoscaling Application Block manages a single instance of Tailspin Surveys.

Tailspin has decided to go ahead and implement option 2. In this model, each data center is self-contained with the Tailspin Surveys application and the Autoscaling Application Block. This makes it easier for Tailspin to manage the different autoscaling requirements of each application block, and minimizes the quantity of data that is moved between data centers. Tailspin will enhance the web-based autoscaling management application to support this scenario.

More Information

For more information about autoscaling and how the Autoscaling Application Block works, see Chapter 4, "Autoscaling and Windows Azure," in this guide.

For instructions about how to install the Tailspin Surveys application, see Appendix B, "Tailspin Surveys Installation Guide."

For more information about the certificates used by the simulated issuers that handle claims-based identity management, see the guide *Developing Applications for the Cloud, 2nd Edition* on MSDN: *http://msdn.microsoft.com/en-us/library/ff966499.aspx*

For more information about the **CloudStorageAccount.Set ConfigurationSettingPublisher** method, see **CloudStorage Account.SetConfigurationSettingPublisher** Method on MSDN: *http://msdn.microsoft.com/en-us/library/microsoft.windowsazure. cloudstorageaccount.setconfigurationsettingpublisher.aspx*

For more information about obtaining an SSL certificate, see "How to Obtain an SSL Certificate" on MSDN: *http://go.microsoft.com/fwlink/?LinkID=234634*

For more information about configuring HTTPS endpoints in Windows Azure web roles, see "How to Configure an SSL Certificate on an HTTPS Endpoint" on MSDN: *http://go.microsoft.com/fwlink/?LinkID=234623*

For more information on management and service certificates in Windows Azure, see "Managing Certificates in Windows Azure" on MSDN: *http://go.microsoft.com/fwlink/?LinkID=234616*

You can use Windows Azure storage analytics to gain deeper insight into your data usage. For more information, see "Storage Analytics Overview" on MSDN: *http://go.microsoft.com/fwlink/?LinkID=234635*

To access web resources more easily, see the online version of the bibliography on MSDN: *http://msdn.microsoft.com/en-us/library/hh749032(v=PandP.50).aspx*

6   Transient Fault Handling

What Are Transient Faults?

When cloud-based applications use other cloud-based services, errors can occur because of temporary conditions such as intermittent service, infrastructure-level faults, or network issues. Very often, if you retry the operation a short time later (maybe only a few milliseconds later) the operation may succeed. These types of error conditions are referred to as transient faults. Transient faults typically occur very infrequently, and in most cases, only a few retries are necessary for the operation to succeed.

Unfortunately, there is no easy way to distinguish transient from non-transient faults; both would most likely result in exceptions being raised in your application. If you retry the operation that causes a non-transient fault (for example a "file not found" error), you most likely get the same exception raised again.

For example, with SQL Azure™ technology platform, one of the important considerations is how you should handle client connections. This is because SQL Azure can use throttling when a client attempts to establish connections to a database or run queries against it. SQL Azure throttles the number of database connections for a variety of reasons, such as excessive resource usage, long-running transactions, and possible failover and load balancing actions. This can lead to the termination of existing client sessions or the temporary inability to establish new connections while the transient conditions persist. SQL Azure can also drop database connections for a variety of reasons related to network connectivity between the client and the remote Microsoft data center: quality of network, intermittent network faults in the client's LAN or WAN infrastructure and other transient technical reasons.

There is no intrinsic way to distinguish between transient and non-transient faults unless the developer of the service explicitly isolated transient faults into a specified subset of exception types or error codes.

Throttling can occur with Windows Azure™ technology platform storage if your client exceeds the scalability targets. For more information, see *"Windows Azure Storage Abstractions and their Scalability Targets."*

Determining which exceptions are the result of transient faults for a service requires detailed knowledge of and experience using the service. The block encapsulates this kind of knowledge and experience for you.

This kind of retry logic is also known as "conditional retry" logic.

What Is the Transient Fault Handling Application Block?

The Transient Fault Handling Application Block makes your application more robust by providing the logic for handling transient faults. It does this in two ways.

First, the block includes logic to identify transient faults for a number of common cloud-based services in the form of detection strategies. These detection strategies contain built-in knowledge that is capable of identifying whether a particular exception is likely to be caused by a transient fault condition.

The block includes detection strategies for the following services:
- SQL Azure
- Windows Azure Service Bus
- Windows Azure Storage Service
- Windows Azure Caching Service

Second, the application block enables you to define your retry strategies so that you can follow a consistent approach to handling transient faults in your applications. The specific retry strategy you use will depend on several factors; for example, how aggressively you want your application to perform retries, and how the service typically behaves when you perform retries. Some services can further throttle or even block client applications that retry too aggressively. A retry strategy defines how many retries you want to make before you decide that the fault is not transient, and what the intervals should be between the retries.

The built-in retry strategies allow you to specify that retries should happen at fixed intervals, at intervals that increase by the same amount each time, and at intervals that increase exponentially but with some random variation. The following table shows examples of all three strategies.

Retry strategy	Example (intervals between retries in seconds)
Fixed interval	2,2,2,2,2,2
Incremental intervals	2,4,6,8,10,12
Random exponential back off intervals	2, 3.755, 9.176, 14.306, 31.895

All retry strategies specify a maximum number of retries after which the original exception is allowed to bubble up to your application.

In many cases, you should use the random exponential back-off strategy to gracefully back off the load on the service. This is especially true if the service is throttling client requests.

You can define your own custom detection strategies if the built-in detection strategies included with the application block do not meet your requirements. The application block also allows you to define your own custom retry strategies that define additional patterns for retry intervals.

Figure 1 illustrates how the key elements of the Transient Fault Handling Application Block work together to enable you to add the retry logic to your application.

High throughput applications should typically use an exponential back-off strategy. However, for user-facing applications such as websites you may want to consider a linear back-off strategy to maintain the responsiveness of the UI.

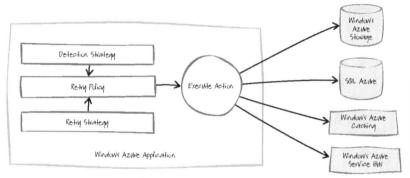

FIGURE 1
The Transient Fault Handling Application Block

A retry policy combines a detection strategy with a retry strategy. You can then use one of the overloaded versions of the **Execute Action** method to wrap the call that your application makes to one of the services.

HISTORICAL NOTE

The Transient Fault Handling Application Block is a product of the collaboration between the *Microsoft patterns & practices* team and the *Windows Azure Customer Advisory Team*. It is based on the initial detection and retry strategies, and the data access support from the "*Transient Fault Handling Framework for SQL Azure, Windows Azure Storage, Service Bus & Cache.*" The new application block now includes enhanced configuration support, enhanced support for wrapping asynchronous calls, provides integration of the application block's retry strategies with the Windows Azure storage retry mechanism, and works with the Enterprise Library dependency injection container. The new Transient Fault Handling Application Block supersedes the Transient Fault Handling Framework and is now the recommended approach to handling transient faults in Windows Azure applications.

You must select the appropriate detection strategy for the service whose method you are calling from your Windows Azure application.

Using the Transient Fault Handling Application Block

This section describes, at a high-level, how to use the Transient Fault Handling Application Block. It is divided into the following main sub-sections. The order of these sections reflects the order in which you would typically perform the associated tasks.

- **Adding the Transient Fault Handling Application Block to your Visual Studio Project**. This section describes how you can prepare your Microsoft Visual Studio® development system solution to use the block.

- **Defining a retry strategy**. This section describes the ways that you can define a retry strategy in your application.

- **Defining a retry policy.** This section describes how you can define a retry policy in your application.

- **Executing an operation with a retry policy**. This section describes how to execute actions with a retry policy to handle any transient faults.

> *A retry policy is the combination of a retry strategy and a detection strategy. You use a retry policy when you execute an operation that may be affected by transient faults.*

For more examples of how you can use the Transient Fault Handling Application Block in your Windows Azure application, see Chapter 7, "Making Tailspin Surveys More Resilient."

For detailed information about configuring the Transient Fault Handling Application Block and writing code that uses the Transient Fault Handling Application Block, see the topic *"The Transient Fault Handling Application Block"* on MSDN®.

ADDING THE TRANSIENT FAULT HANDLING APPLICATION BLOCK TO YOUR VISUAL STUDIO PROJECT

As a developer, before you can write any code that uses the Transient Fault Handling Application Block, you must configure your Visual Studio project with all of the necessary assemblies, references, and other resources that you'll need. For information about how you can use NuGet to prepare your Visual Studio project to work with the Transient Fault Handling Application Block, see the topic *"Adding the Transient Fault Handling Application Block to your Solution"* on MSDN.

NuGet makes it very easy for you to configure your project with all of the prerequisites for using the Transient Fault Handling Application Block.

INSTANTIATING THE TRANSIENT FAULT HANDLING APPLICATION BLOCK OBJECTS

There are two basic approaches to instantiating the objects from the application block that your application requires. In the first approach, you can explicitly instantiate all the objects in code, as shown in the following code snippet:

```csharp
C#
var retryStrategy = new Incremental(5, TimeSpan.FromSeconds(1),
  TimeSpan.FromSeconds(2));

var retryPolicy =
new RetryPolicy<StorageTransientErrorDetectionStrategy>
                                    (retryStrategy);
```

> *If you instantiate the* **RetryPolicy** *object using* **new***, you cannot use the default strategies defined in the configuration.*

In the second approach, you can use the Enterprise Library infrastructure to instantiate and manage the objects for you as shown in the following code snippet:

```csharp
C#
var retryManager = EnterpriseLibraryContainer.Current
                .GetInstance<RetryManager>();

var retryPolicy = retryManager.GetRetryPolicy
    <StorageTransientErrorDetectionStrategy>("Incremental Retry
                                    Strategy");
```

There is an additional approach that is provided for backward compatibility with the *"Transient Fault Handling Application Framework"* that uses the **RetryPolicyFactory** class:

```csharp
C#
var retryPolicy = RetryPolicyFactory.GetRetryPolicy
    <StorageTransientErrorDetectionStrategy>("Incremental Retry
                                    Strategy");
```

DEFINING A RETRY STRATEGY

There are three considerations in defining retry strategies for your application: which retry strategy to use, where to define the retry strategy, and whether to use default retry strategies.

In most cases, you should use one of the built-in retry strategies: fixed interval, incremental, or random exponential back off. You configure each of these strategies using custom sets of parameters to meet your application's requirements; the parameters specify when the strategy should stop retrying an operation, and what the intervals between the retries should be. The choice of retry strategy will be largely determined by the specific requirements of your application. For more details about the parameters for each retry strategy, see the topic *"Source Schema for the Transient Fault Handling Application Block"* on MSDN.

You can define your own custom retry strategy. For more information, see the topic *"Implementing a Custom Retry Strategy"* on MSDN.

You can define your retry policies either in code or in the application configuration file. Defining your retry policies in code is most appropriate for small applications with a limited number of calls that require retry logic. Defining the retry policies in configuration is more useful if you have a large number of operations that require retry logic, because it makes it easier to maintain and modify the policies.

For more information about how to define your retry strategy in code, see the topic *"Specifying Retry Strategies in Code"* on MSDN.

For more information about how to define your retry strategies in a configuration file, see the topic *"Specifying Retry Strategies in the Configuration"* on MSDN.

If you define your retry strategies in the configuration file for the application, you can also define default retry strategies. The block allows you to specify default retry strategies at two levels. You can specify a default retry strategy for each of the following operation categories: SQL connection operations, SQL command operations, Windows Azure Service Bus operations, Windows Azure caching, and Windows Azure storage operations. You can also specify a global default retry strategy.

DEFINING A RETRY POLICY

A retry policy is the combination of a retry strategy and a detection strategy that you use when you execute an operation that may be affected by transient faults. The **RetryManager** class includes methods that enable you to create retry policies by explicitly identifying the retry strategy and detection strategy, or by using default retry strategies defined in the configuration file.

For more information about using the retry policies, see the topic *"Key Scenarios"* on MSDN.

For more information about the **RetryPolicy** delegate in the **Microsoft.WindowsAzure.StorageClient** namespace, see the blog post *"Overview of Retry Policies in the Windows Azure Storage Client Library."*

If you are using Windows Azure storage and you are already using the retry policies mechanism in the **Microsoft.WindowsAzure. StorageClient** namespace, then you can use retry strategies from the block and configure the Windows Azure storage client API to take advantage of the extensible retry functionality provided by the block.

EXECUTING AN OPERATION WITH A RETRY POLICY

The **RetryPolicy** class includes several overloaded versions of the **ExecuteAction** method. You use the **ExecuteAction** method to wrap the calls in your application that may be affected by transient faults. The different overloaded versions enable you to wrap the following types of calls to a service.

- Synchronous calls that return a **void**.
- Synchronous calls that return a value.
- Asynchronous calls that return a **void**.
- Asynchronous calls that return a value.

The **ExecuteAction** method automatically applies the configured retry strategy and detection strategy when it invokes the specified action. If no transient fault manifests itself during the invocation, your application continues as normal, as if there was nothing between your code and the action being invoked. If a transient fault does manifest itself, the block will initiate the recovery by attempting to invoke the specified action multiple times as defined in the retry strategy. As soon as a retry attempt succeeds, your application continues as normal. If the block does not succeed in executing the operation within the number of retries specified by the retry strategy, then the block rethrows the exception to your application. Your application must still handle this exception properly.

You can use the **Retrying** event to receive notifications in your application about the retry operations that the block performs.

If you are working with SQL Azure, the block includes classes that provide direct support for SQL Azure, such as the **ReliableSqlConnection** class. These classes will help you reduce the amount of code you need to write.

> *The Transient Fault Handling Application Block is not a substitute for proper exception handling. Your application must still handle any exceptions that are thrown by the service you are using.*

In addition, the application block includes classes that wrap many common SQL Azure operations with a retry policy for you. Using these classes minimizes the amount of code you need to write.

For more information about executing an operation with a retry policy, see the topic *"Key Scenarios"* on MSDN.

When Should You Use the Transient Fault Handling Application Block?

This section describes two scenarios in which you should consider using the Transient Fault Handling Application Block in your Windows Azure solution.

You are Using a Windows Azure Service

If your application uses any of the Windows Azure services supported by the Transient Fault Handling Application Block (SQL Azure, Windows Azure Storage, Windows Azure Caching, or Windows Azure Service Bus), then you can make your application more robust by using the application block. Any Windows Azure application that uses these services may occasionally encounter transient faults with these services. Although you could add your own detection logic to your application, the application block's built-in detection strategies will handle a wider range of transient faults. It is also quicker and easier to use the application block instead of developing your own solution.

The Windows Azure storage client API already includes support for custom retry policies. You can use retry strategies from the application block with the Windows Azure storage client API. Using retry strategies from the Transient Fault Handling Application Block with the Windows Azure retry mechanism enables you to use the built-in and custom retry strategies and to support defining retry strategies in the application configuration.

> *Using Transient Fault Handling Application Block retry polices instead of Windows Azure built-in retry policies will enable you to take advantage of the customizable and extensible retry logic in the application block.*

For more information about retries in Windows Azure storage, see *"Overview of Retry Policies in the Windows Azure Storage Client Library."*

You Are Using a Custom Service

If your application uses a custom service, it can still benefit from using the Transient Fault Handling Application Block. You can author a custom detection strategy for your service that encapsulates your knowledge of which transient exceptions may result from a service invocation. The Transient Fault Handling Application Block then provides you with the framework for defining retry policies and for wrapping your method calls so that the application block applies the retry logic.

More Information

For more examples of how you can use the Transient Fault Handling Application Block in your Windows Azure application, see Chapter 7, "Making Tailspin Surveys More Resilient."

For detailed information about configuring the Transient Fault Handling Application Block and writing code that uses the Transient Fault Handling Application Block, see the topic "The Transient Fault Handling Application Block" on MSDN:
http://msdn.microsoft.com/en-us/library/hh680934(v=PandP.50).aspx

For more information about throttling in Windows Azure, see "Windows Azure Storage Abstractions and their Scalability Targets" on MSDN:
http://go.microsoft.com/fwlink/?LinkID=234633

For information about how you can use NuGet to prepare your Visual Studio project to work with the Transient Fault Handling Application Block, see the topic "Adding the Transient Fault Handling Application Block to your Solution" on MSDN:
http://msdn.microsoft.com/en-us/library/hh680891(v=PandP.50).aspx

There is an additional approach that is provided for backward compatibility with the "Transient Fault Handling Application Framework" that uses the **RetryPolicyFactory** class:
http://windowsazurecat.com/2011/02/transient-fault-handling-framework/

For more details about the parameters for each retry strategy, see the topic "Source Schema for the Transient Fault Handling Application Block" on MSDN:
http://msdn.microsoft.com/en-us/library/hh680941(v=PandP.50).aspx

You can define your own, custom retry strategy. For more information, see the topic "Implementing a Custom Retry Strategy" on MSDN:
http://msdn.microsoft.com/en-us/library/hh680943(v=PandP.50).aspx

For more information about how to define your retry strategy in code, see the topic "Specifying Retry Strategies in Code" on MSDN:
http://msdn.microsoft.com/en-us/library/hh680927(v=PandP.50).aspx

For more information about how to define your retry strategies in a configuration file, see the topic "Specifying Retry Strategies in the Configuration" on MSDN:
http://msdn.microsoft.com/en-us/library/hh680900(v=PandP.50).aspx

For more information about using the retry policies, see the topic "Key Scenarios" on MSDN:
http://msdn.microsoft.com/en-us/library/hh680948(v=PandP.50).aspx

For more information about the **RetryPolicy** delegate in the **Microsoft.WindowsAzure.StorageClient** namespace, see the blog post "Overview of Retry Policies in the Windows Azure Storage Client Library":
http://go.microsoft.com/fwlink/?LinkID=234630

For more information about retries in Windows Azure storage, see "Overview of Retry Policies in the Windows Azure Storage Client Library":
http://go.microsoft.com/fwlink/?LinkID=234630

The Transient Fault Handling Application Block is a product of the collaboration between the Microsoft patterns & practices team (*http://msdn.microsoft.com/practices*) and the Windows Azure Customer Advisory Team (*http://windowsazurecat.com/index.php*). It is based on the initial detection and retry strategies, and the data access support from the "Transient Fault Handling Framework for SQL Azure, Windows Azure Storage, Service Bus & Cache" on MSDN:
http://windowsazurecat.com/2011/02/transient-fault-handling-framework/

To access web resources more easily, see the online version of the bibliography on MSDN:
http://msdn.microsoft.com/en-us/library/hh749032(v=PandP.50).aspx

7   Making Tailspin Surveys More Resilient

This chapter walks you through the changes that Tailspin made when it added the Transient Fault Handling Application Block to the Surveys application in order to improve the resilience of the application to transient fault conditions in the Windows Azure™ technology platform environment.

The Premise

In order to meet the requirements of its larger customers, Tailspin agreed to increase the service levels in their service-level agreements (SLAs), especially with regards to the reliability and availability of the Surveys application. These customers also have more stringent performance requirements—for example, the maximum time the data export to SQL Azure™ technology platform should take. To meet these new SLA requirements, Tailspin closely re-examined the Surveys application to see where it could improve the application's resilience.

Tailspin discovered that when the Surveys application makes calls to SQL Azure or Windows Azure Storage, transient conditions sometimes cause errors. The call succeeds if Tailspin retries the operation a short time later, when the transient condition has cleared.

The Tailspin Surveys application uses Windows Azure storage and SQL Azure. Survey definitions are stored in Windows Azure tables, customer configuration data is stored in Windows Azure blob storage, and survey answers are also stored in Windows Azure blob storage. The Surveys application also enables customers to export survey data to SQL Azure where customers can perform their own detailed analysis of the results. For some customers, the SQL Azure instance is located in a different data center from where the customer's surveys are hosted.

Operators have noticed occasional errors in the Surveys application log files that relate to storage errors. These errors are not related to specific areas of functionality, but appear to occur at random.

Applications that run on the Windows Azure platform must be able to handle transient fault conditions gracefully and efficiently in order to reduce the potential impact of transient conditions on the application's stability.

Improving the reliability and resilience of Surveys is vital if Tailspin is going to succeed in attracting larger customers.

There have been a small number of reports that users creating new surveys have lost the survey definition when they clicked the Save button in the user interface (UI).

There have also been occasions when long-running jobs that export data to SQL Azure have failed. Because there is no resume method for partially completed export tasks, Tailspin must restart the export process from the beginning. Tailspin has rerun the jobs they have not completed successfully, but this has meant that Tailspin has failed to meet its SLA with the customer. Where the export is to a different data center than the one that hosts the survey definitions, Tailspin has incurred additional bandwidth-related costs as a result of having to rerun the export job.

Goals and Requirements

Tailspin wants to implement automatic retry logic for all of its Windows Azure storage operations to improve the overall reliability of the application. It wants to minimize the risk of losing survey data and creating inaccurate statistics. Tailspin wants to ensure that the application is as resilient as possible, so that it can recover from any transient errors without operator intervention. It also wants to minimize the chance of customers experiencing errors when they are creating new survey definitions.

Tailspin also wants to improve the reliability of the export tasks that send data to SQL Azure so that it can meet its SLAs with its customers.

Tailspin wants to be able to tune the retry policies (for example, by adjusting the back-off delay), in different scenarios. Some tasks are more time critical, such as saving a new survey definition where a user is waiting for an acknowledgement that the definition has been saved; other tasks are less time critical, such as the statistics calculation, which is not designed to give real-time results.

Overview of the Transient Fault Handling Application Block Solution

The Transient Fault Handling Application Block enables you to add retry logic to your cloud-based application. You can use the application block to apply a retry policy to any calls that may experience errors as a result of transient conditions.

The Transient Fault Handling Application Block includes detection strategies that can identify exceptions that may be caused by transient faults. Tailspin Surveys uses Windows Azure storage and SQL Azure; the Transient Fault Handling Application Block includes detection strategies for these services.

The Transient Fault Handling Application Block uses retry strategies to define retry patterns: the number of retries and the interval between them. These retry strategies can be defined in code or in configuration. Tailspin plans to use retry strategies defined in configuration so that it is easier to tune the behavior of the retry strategies used by the Surveys application.

Inside the Implementation

This section describes some of the details of how Tailspin uses the Transient Fault Handling Application Block and how it modified the Surveys application to use the application block. If you are not interested in the details, you can skip to the next section.

You may find it useful to have the Tailspin solution open in Visual Studio while you read this section so that you can refer to the code directly.

For instructions on installing the Tailspin Surveys application, see Appendix B, "Tailspin Surveys Installation Guide."

Tailspin uses the Transient Fault Handling Application Block in the Surveys application wherever it is using the Windows Azure storage API or invoking an operation on a SQL Azure database. For example, it uses the application block in the code that accesses the rule and service information stores, in the wrapper classes for the Windows Azure storage types, and in the **SurveySqlStore** class. All of these classes are located in the **Tailspin.Shared** project.

The configuration file for each worker and web role in the Surveys application includes the retry strategies shown in the following code snippet.

XML

```
<RetryPolicyConfiguration
    defaultRetryStrategy="Fixed Interval Retry Strategy"
    defaultAzureStorageRetryStrategy="Fixed Interval Retry
                            Strategy"
    defaultSqlCommandRetryStrategy="Backoff Retry Strategy">
  <incremental name="Incremental Retry Strategy"
            retryIncrement="00:00:01"
            initialInterval="00:00:01"
            maxRetryCount="10" />
  <fixedInterval name="Fixed Interval Retry Strategy"
            retryInterval="00:00:05"
            maxRetryCount="6"
            firstFastRetry="true" />
  <exponentialBackoff name="Backoff Retry Strategy"
                minBackoff="00:00:05"
                maxBackoff="00:00:45"
```

```
                    deltaBackoff="00:00:04"
                    maxRetryCount="10" />
</RetryPolicyConfiguration>
```

Tailspin uses the Enterprise Library configuration tool to edit these settings.

Tailspin uses the **RetryManager** class to load the retry strategies from the configuration file and instantiate a retry policy. The following code snippet from the **RuleSetModelStore** class shows an example of how Tailspin creates a new retry policy that uses the Windows Azure storage detection strategy and the "Incremental Retry Strategy" from the configuration.

```C#
public RuleSetModelStore(
    RuleSetModelToXmlElementConverter
        ruleSetModelToXmlElementConverter,
    [Dependency("RuleSetModel")] IConfigurationFileAccess
                                    fileAccess,
    RetryManager retryManager)
{
    this.retryPolicy = retryManager.GetRetryPolicy
      <StorageTransientErrorDetectionStrategy>
      (AzureConstants.FaultHandlingPolicies.Incremental);

    ...
}
```

*You should be careful of trying to load retry strategies from the web.config file by using the **RetryPolicyFactory** or **Retry Manager** classes in the web role **OnStart** event. See the topic "Specifying Retry Strategies in the Configuration" on MSDN for more details.*

If you are using the Transient Fault Handling Application Block with Windows Azure storage, you should be careful not to use the built-in retry policies in the Windows Azure storage APIs. The following code snippet from the **AzureQueue** class in the **Tailspin.Shared** project shows how Tailspin disables the built-in retry policies.

```C#
var client = this.account.CreateCloudQueueClient();
client.RetryPolicy = RetryPolicies.NoRetry();
```

The following code snippet from the **GetFileContent** method in the **RuleModelStore** class shows how Tailspin wraps a call that accesses Windows Azure storage that may be affected by transient fault conditions with the retry policy.

```
C#
try
{
    return this.retryPolicy.ExecuteAction(
        () => this.fileAccess.GetFileContent());
}
catch (ConfigurationFileAccessException)
{
    return null;
}
```

Tailspin uses the same approach when the Surveys application saves data to SQL Azure, as shown in the following code sample from the **SurveySqlStore** class. This example also shows how to load a default policy from configuration.

```
C#
public SurveySqlStore()
{
    this.retryPolicy =
        RetryPolicyFactory.GetDefaultSqlCommandRetryPolicy();
}
public void SaveSurvey(string connectionString,
                    SurveyData surveyData)
{
    using (var dataContext =
        new SurveySqlDataContext(connectionString))
    {
        dataContext.SurveyDatas.InsertOnSubmit(surveyData);
        try
        {
            this.retryPolicy.ExecuteAction(() => dataContext
                                        .SubmitChanges());
        }
        catch (SqlException ex)
        {
            Trace.TraceError(ex.TraceInformation());
            throw;
        }
    }
}
```

If Tailspin wanted to collect information about the retries in the application, it could use the **Retrying** event in the retry policy to capture the details and log them for analysis.

Tailspin Surveys uses LINQ to SQL as an object relational mapper. All database interactions are abstracted by the data model; therefore, Tailspin does not have to use the **ReliableSqlConnection** class or the SQL Azure extension classes provided by the Transient Fault Handling Application Block.

Tailspin's data access requirements are relatively simple, so it only needs to use the simplest version of the **ExecuteAction** method. It does not need to wrap any calls that return values or make any asynchronous calls.

Setup and Physical Deployment

The Tailspin Surveys application uses retry strategies defined in the configuration files for the roles that use Windows Azure storage and SQL Azure. In the sample, all of these roles use the same retry strategies. In a real-world deployment you should adjust the retry strategies to meet the specific requirements of your application.

More Information

For instructions on installing the Tailspin Surveys application, see Appendix B, "Tailspin Surveys Installation Guide" on MSDN:
http://msdn.microsoft.com/en-us/library/hh680894(v=PandP.50).aspx

For more information about retry strategies, see "Specifying Retry Strategies in the Configuration" on MSDN:
http://msdn.microsoft.com/en-us/library/hh680900(v=PandP.50).aspx

To access web resources more easily, see the online version of the bibliography on MSDN:
http://msdn.microsoft.com/en-us/library/hh749032(v=PandP.50).aspx

APPENDIX A

Sample Configurations for Deploying Tailspin Surveys to Multiple Data Centers

This appendix contains sample service information and rules definitions for the two alternative architectures for Tailspin's autoscaling infrastructure described in Chapter 5, "Making Tailspin Surveys More Elastic."

Option 1

Option 1 deploys the management application and the Autoscaling Application Block to the North Central US data center only.

SERVICE MODEL

```XML
<?xml version="1.0" encoding="utf-8"?>
<serviceModel ...>
  <subscriptions>
    <subscription name="Tailspin Surveys Production"
                  subscriptionId="..."
                  certificateThumbprint="..."
                  certificateStoreName="My"
                  certificateStoreLocation="LocalMachine">
      <services>
      <!--
        Multiple service definitions, one for each data center that
        Tailspin Surveys is deployed to.
        Note: All share the same wadStorageAccountName values because the
        diagnostic is collected centrally in this model.
      -->
      <service dnsPrefix="ustailspinsurveys" slot="Production" scalingMode="Scale">
        <roles>
          <role alias="usTailSpinWorkersSurveys"
            roleName="TailSpin.Workers.Surveys"
```

```
          wadStorageAccountName="usTailspin" />
        <role alias="usTailSpinWebSurveyPublic"
          roleName="TailSpin.Web.Survey.Public"
          wadStorageAccountName="usTailspin" />
        <role alias="usTailSpinWeb"
          roleName="TailSpin.Web"
          wadStorageAccountName="usTailspin" />
      </roles>
    </service>
    <service dnsPrefix="eutailspinsurveys" slot="Production" scalingMode="Scale">
      <roles>
        <role alias="euTailSpinWorkersSurveys"
          roleName="TailSpin.Workers.Surveys"
          wadStorageAccountName="euTailspin" />
        <role alias="euTailSpinWebSurveyPublic"
          roleName="TailSpin.Web.Survey.Public"
          wadStorageAccountName="euTailspin" />
        <role alias="euTailSpinWeb"
          roleName="TailSpin.Web"
          wadStorageAccountName="euTailspin" />
      </roles>
    </service>
    <service dnsPrefix="astailspinsurveys" slot="Production" scalingMode="Scale">
      <roles>
        <role alias="asTailSpinWorkersSurveys"
          roleName="TailSpin.Workers.Surveys"
          wadStorageAccountName="asTailspin" />
        <role alias="asTailSpinWebSurveyPublic"
          roleName="TailSpin.Web.Survey.Public"
          wadStorageAccountName="asTailspin" />
        <role alias="asTailSpinWeb"
          roleName="TailSpin.Web"
          wadStorageAccountName="asTailspin" />
      </roles>
    </service>
  </services>
  <!--
    Multiple storage accounts, one for each data center that Tailspin Surveys
    is deployed to. Each storage account has its own connection string.
    These queues are used by the Tailspin Surveys application and are
    included here because we want to use rules that monitor the queue lengths.
  -->
  <storageAccounts>
    <storageAccount alias="usTailspin" connectionString="...">
      <queues>
```

```xml
            <queue alias="usTailspinSurveyAnswerStoredQueue"
              queueName="surveyanswerstored" />
            <queue alias="usTailspinSurveyTransferQueue"
              queueName="surveytransfer" />
          </queues>
        </storageAccount>
        <storageAccount alias="euTailspin" connectionString="...">
          <queues>
            <queue alias="euTailspinSurveyAnswerStoredQueue"
              queueName="surveyanswerstored" />
            <queue alias="euTailspinSurveyTransferQueue"
              queueName="surveytransfer" />
          </queues>
        </storageAccount>
        <storageAccount alias="asTailspin" connectionString="...">
          <queues>
            <queue alias="asTailspinSurveyAnswerStoredQueue"
              queueName="surveyanswerstored" />
            <queue alias="asTailspinSurveyTransferQueue"
              queueName="surveytransfer" />
          </queues>
        </storageAccount>
      </storageAccounts>
    </subscription>
  </subscriptions>
  <scaleGroups />
</serviceModel>
```

Rules

```xml
<?xml version="1.0" encoding="utf-16"?>
<rules ...>
  <constraintRules>
    <!--
      An example constraint rule - there are more.
      We need duplicates of the same rule because the utcOffset values are different.
      In some cases it may be possible to use the same rule with an action for each
      region.
    -->
    <rule name="US WorkerRole reserving instances for midnight survey processing"
      description="..." enabled="true" rank="5">
      <timetable startDate="2011-10-05" endDate="2012-10-06" startTime="00:01:00"
        duration="02:00:00" utcOffset="-08:00">
        <daily />
```

```
      </timetable>
      <actions>
        <range target="usTailSpinWorkersSurveys" min="3" max="6" />
      </actions>
    </rule>
    <rule name="EU WorkerRole reserving instances for midnight survey processing"
      description="..." enabled="true" rank="5">
      <timetable startDate="2011-10-05" endDate="2012-10-06" startTime="00:01:00"
        duration="02:00:00" utcOffset="+00:00">
        <daily />
      </timetable>
      <actions>
        <range target="euTailSpinWorkersSurveys" min="3" max="6" />
      </actions>
    </rule>
    <rule name="ASIA WorkerRole reserving instances for midnight survey processing"
      description="..." enabled="true" rank="5">
      <timetable startDate="2011-10-05" endDate="2012-10-06" startTime="00:01:00"
        duration="02:00:00" utcOffset="+09:00">
        <daily />
      </timetable>
      <actions>
        <range target="asTailSpinWorkersSurveys" min="3" max="6" />
      </actions>
    </rule>
</constraintRules>


<reactiveRules>
  <!--
    An example reactive rule - there are more.
    We need duplicates of the same rule because we must tie the operand source to
    the correct target.
  -->
  <rule name="US Heavy demand on public site" description="..." enabled="true">
    <actions>
      <scale target="usTailSpinWebSurveyPublic" by="1" />
    </actions>
    <when>
      <greater operand="usASPNET_requests_rejected" than="5" />
    </when>
    <rank>0</rank>
  </rule>
  <rule name="EU Heavy demand on public site" description="..." enabled="true">
```

```xml
    <actions>
      <scale target="euTailSpinWebSurveyPublic" by="1" />
    </actions>
    <when>
      <greater operand="euASPNET_requests_rejected" than="5" />
    </when>
    <rank>0</rank>
  </rule>
  <rule name="AS Heavy demand on public site" description="..." enabled="true">
    <actions>
      <scale target="asTailSpinWebSurveyPublic" by="1" />
    </actions>
    <when>
      <greater operand="asASPNET_requests_rejected" than="5" />
    </when>
    <rank>0</rank>
  </rule>
</reactiveRules>

<operands>
  <!-- Operands for US roles -->
  <performanceCounter alias="usASPNET_requests_rejected" timespan="00:10:00"
    aggregate="Average" source="usTailSpinWebSurveyPublic"
    performanceCounterName="\ASP.NET\Requests Rejected" />
  <performanceCounter alias="usCPU_over_20_minutes_for_TailspinWeb"
    timespan="00:20:00" aggregate="Average" source="usTailSpinWeb"
    performanceCounterName="\Processor(_Total)\% Processor Time" />
  <performanceCounter alias="usCPU_over_30_minutes" timespan="00:30:00"
    aggregate="Average" source="usTailSpinWorkersSurveys"
    performanceCounterName="\Processor(_Total)\% Processor Time" />

  <!-- Operands for EU roles -->
  <performanceCounter alias="euASPNET_requests_rejected" timespan="00:10:00"
    aggregate="Average" source="euTailSpinWebSurveyPublic"
    performanceCounterName="\ASP.NET\Requests Rejected" />
  <performanceCounter alias="euCPU_over_20_minutes_for_TailspinWeb"
    timespan="00:20:00" aggregate="Average" source="euTailSpinWeb"
    performanceCounterName="\Processor(_Total)\% Processor Time" />
  <performanceCounter alias="euCPU_over_30_minutes" timespan="00:30:00"
    aggregate="Average" source="euTailSpinWorkersSurveys"
    performanceCounterName="\Processor(_Total)\% Processor Time" />

  <!-- Operands for Asia roles -->
  <performanceCounter alias="asASPNET_requests_rejected" timespan="00:10:00"
    aggregate="Average" source="asTailSpinWebSurveyPublic"
```

```
        performanceCounterName="\ASP.NET\Requests Rejected" />
    <performanceCounter alias="asCPU_over_20_minutes_for_TailspinWeb"
      timespan="00:20:00" aggregate="Average" source="asTailSpinWeb"
      performanceCounterName="\Processor(_Total)\% Processor Time" />
    <performanceCounter alias="asCPU_over_30_minutes" timespan="00:30:00"
      aggregate="Average" source="asTailSpinWorkersSurveys"
      performanceCounterName="\Processor(_Total)\% Processor Time" />

    <!-- Custom operands - require an attribute to specify the hosted service -->
    <activeSurveysOperand alias="usNumberOfSurveysSubmitted" timespan="00:10:00"
      aggregate="Average" minNumberOfAnswers="0" hostedService="USTailspin"
      xmlns="http://Tailspin/ActiveSurveys" />
    <tenantCountOperand alias="usNumberOfTenants" timespan="00:10:00"
      aggregate="Average" hostedService="USTailspin"
      xmlns="http://Tailspin/TenantCount" />

    <activeSurveysOperand alias="euNumberOfSurveysSubmitted" timespan="00:10:00"
      aggregate="Average" minNumberOfAnswers="0" hostedService="EUTailspin"
      xmlns="http://Tailspin/ActiveSurveys" />
    <tenantCountOperand alias="euNumberOfTenants" timespan="00:10:00"
      aggregate="Average" hostedService="EUTailspin"
      xmlns="http://Tailspin/TenantCount" />

    <activeSurveysOperand alias="asNumberOfSurveysSubmitted" timespan="00:10:00"
      aggregate="Average" minNumberOfAnswers="0" hostedService="ASTailspin"
      xmlns="http://Tailspin/ActiveSurveys" />
    <tenantCountOperand alias="asNumberOfTenants" timespan="00:10:00"
      aggregate="Average" hostedService="ASTailspin"
      xmlns="http://Tailspin/TenantCount" />

  </operands>
</rules>
```

Option 2

Option 2 deploys the management application to the North Central US data center only and the Autoscaling Application Block to each data center. Each data center has its own service model definition and rule set.

SERVICE MODEL

```xml
XML
<?xml version="1.0" encoding="utf-8"?>
<serviceModel ...>
  <subscriptions>
    <subscription name="Tailspin Surveys Production"
                  subscriptionId="..."
                  certificateThumbprint="..."
                  certificateStoreName="My"
                  certificateStoreLocation="LocalMachine">
      <services>
        <!--
          Single service definitions.
          Each data center has a copy of this model with the dnsPrefix changed to
          reflect the data center location.
        -->
        <service dnsPrefix="ustailspinsurveys" slot="Production" scalingMode="Scale">
          <roles>
            <role alias="TailSpinWorkersSurveys" roleName="TailSpin.Workers.Surveys"
              wadStorageAccountName="Tailspin" />
            <role alias="TailSpinWebSurveyPublic"
              roleName="TailSpin.Web.Survey.Public"
              wadStorageAccountName="Tailspin" />
            <role alias="TailSpinWeb" roleName="TailSpin.Web"
              wadStorageAccountName="Tailspin" />
          </roles>
        </service>
      </services>
      <!--
        Single storage account, duplicated in each data center.
        Each data center will have a different
        connectionString for its storage account.
      -->
      <storageAccounts>
        <storageAccount alias="Tailspin" connectionString="...">
          <queues>
            <queue alias="TailspinSurveyAnswerStoredQueue"
              queueName="surveyanswerstored" />
            <queue alias="TailspinSurveyTransferQueue" queueName="surveytransfer" />
          </queues>
        </storageAccount>
      </storageAccounts>
    </subscription>
  </subscriptions>
  <scaleGroups />
</serviceModel>
```

Rules

```XML
<?xml version="1.0" encoding="utf-16"?>
<rules ...>
  <constraintRules>
    <!--
      An example constraint rule - there are more.
      Each region has its own rules file - it must be edited to reflect the different
      utcOffset values.
    -->
    <rule name="WorkerRole reserving instances for midnight survey processing"
         description="..." enabled="true" rank="5">
      <timetable startDate="2011-10-05" endDate="2012-10-06" startTime="00:01:00"
                 duration="02:00:00" utcOffset="-08:00">
        <daily />
      </timetable>
      <actions>
        <range target="TailSpinWorkersSurveys" min="3" max="6" />
      </actions>
    </rule>
  </constraintRules>


  <reactiveRules>
    <!--
      An example reactive rule - there are more.
      Each region can have the same reactive rules, although you may want to change
      them in each region to reflect different usage patterns.
    -->
    <rule name="Heavy demand on public site" description="..." enabled="true">
      <actions>
        <scale target="TailSpinWebSurveyPublic" by="1" />
      </actions>
      <when>
        <greater operand="ASPNET_requests_rejected" than="5" />
      </when>
      <rank>0</rank>
    </rule>

  </reactiveRules>
```

```xml
<operands>
  <!-- Operands can be identical for the different regions -->
  <performanceCounter alias="ASPNET_requests_rejected" timespan="00:10:00"
    aggregate="Average" source="TailSpinWebSurveyPublic"
    performanceCounterName="\ASP.NET\Requests Rejected" />
  <performanceCounter alias="CPU_over_20_minutes_for_TailspinWeb"
    timespan="00:20:00" aggregate="Average" source="TailSpinWeb"
    performanceCounterName="\Processor(_Total)\% Processor Time" />
  <performanceCounter alias="CPU_over_30_minutes" timespan="00:30:00"
    aggregate="Average" source="TailSpinWorkersSurveys"
    performanceCounterName="\Processor(_Total)\% Processor Time" />

  <activeSurveysOperand alias="NumberOfSurveysSubmitted" timespan="00:10:00"
    aggregate="Average" minNumberOfAnswers="0"
    xmlns="http://Tailspin/ActiveSurveys" />
  <tenantCountOperand alias="NumberOfTenants" timespan="00:10:00"
    aggregate="Average" xmlns="http://Tailspin/TenantCount" />
</operands>

</rules>
```

APPENDIX B

Tailspin Surveys Installation Guide

Introduction

This document will guide you through the installation of the Tailspin Surveys application for Microsoft® Enterprise Library 5.0 Integration Pack for Windows Azure, including the Autoscaling Application Block ("WASABi") and the Transient Fault Handing Application Block ("Topaz"). The Surveys application is a comprehensive sample application that demonstrates how you can use the Autoscaling Application Block to scale an application running on Windows Azure™ technology platform up or down elastically, based on the rules you specify. In addition, it contains an example of a management site that you can use to configure service information and rules that are used by the Autoscaling Application Block to monitor how the application's role instances change based on the rules and the conditions causing the changes.

The Tailspin Surveys application covers a few scenarios and features, but it does not cover the many other useful features of the Autoscaling Application Block or the Transient Fault Handing Application Block or the many possible scenarios in which you will benefit from their use. Therefore, we strongly encourage you to go beyond the basic uses of the application blocks demonstrated in the Tailspin Surveys application. For comprehensive coverage of the application blocks, see *"The Autoscaling Application Block"* and *"The Transient Fault Handling Application Block."*

This version of the Tailspin Surveys application builds on the previous releases of the Surveys application by *Microsoft patterns & practices*. Please refer to the installation documents of the *previous releases* for the topics that are not covered in this document.

Installing this application can take between an hour and an hour and a half, depending on your software and hardware configuration and your experience with Windows Azure. This document walks you through the following:

- Installing the required dependencies using the included Dependency checking tool.
- Creating two hosted services for the Tailspin Surveys web application and the Tailspin Surveys autoscaling runtime and management application.
- Updating the project files with your Windows Azure subscription information.
- Deploying the application to Windows Azure.
- Verifying the installation on Windows Azure.

PREREQUISITES

In order to run the Tailspin Surveys application, you will need the following:

- A development machine running Microsoft Visual Studio® 2010 development system SP1.
- All required Microsoft Windows® updates.
- *NuGet Package Manager (http://nuget.codeplex.com/).*
- A Windows Azure subscription with room for two hosted services (if you want to run the Tailspin Surveys application and the Autoscaler component with the Management Web application in Windows Azure).
- A Windows Azure storage account.
- The Dependency checking tool, discussed below, which will verify that you have the prerequisites listed below installed. If not, it will help you install them.
  - Visual Studio 2010
  - MVC 3 Framework
  - Windows Azure SDK for .NET and Windows Azure Tools for Microsoft Visual Studio – November 2011 Release
  - Windows Identity Foundation Runtime
  - Optional: Microsoft Internet Information Services 7 (IIS)
    - This is required to run the management site in simulated mode or to deploy the Autoscaler locally.

INSTALL SOURCE CODE AND DEPENDENCIES

The Dependency checking tool will check to see if you have the required prerequisites and, if not, will help you install them.

**TO INSTALL THE TAILSPIN SURVEYS APPLICATION
SOURCE CODE AND DEPENDENCIES**

1. Unzip the source code to a location on your hard drive.

   Note: *You should not place the source code in a folder that is nested too deeply, because the Windows Azure Tools for Visual Studio do not support paths that are longer than 255 characters. We have tested the Tailspin Surveys application deployment from C:\Tailspin.*

2. Run "CheckDependencies.cmd" located in the root of your download folder.

3. In the Dependency checking tool, click the **Scan** button.

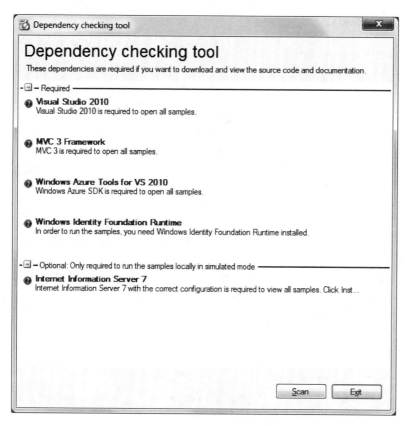

4. Ensure that all the required dependencies have been installed. If not, install each prerequisite one at a time and click the **Rescan** button.

Prepare Your Windows Azure Subscription for Deployment

In order to prepare your Windows Azure subscription for deployment, you will need to do the following:

1. Generate the Windows Azure management certificate and export it.

2. Generate the SSL certificate.

3. Create the required hosted services.

4. Upload the certificates as hosted services' service certificates.

5. Create the storage account.

The sections below will walk you through each of these tasks.

GENERATE THE WINDOWS AZURE MANAGEMENT CERTIFICATE AND EXPORT AS .PFX FILE

The Enterprise Library Autoscaling Application Block needs to use a valid management certificate for your Windows Azure subscription in order to be able to scale your application. If you do not already have a management certificate, you can follow the steps below to generate one. You will also need to upload to the Windows Azure Management Portal the generated management certificate and an SSL certificate, which will be generated in the next steps. In summary, the following steps will allow you to:

- Generate the management certificate.
- Export from Current User\My store to upload to the Windows Azure Management Portal.
- Generate the SSL certificate to upload to the Windows Azure Management Portal.

  You should be aware of the following with respect to certificates:
- Windows Azure roles that expose SSL endpoints or affect changes to Windows Azure deployments, such as the Autoscaling Block, require access to the related certificates from within the running instances of those roles. These certificates need to be uploaded to the Service Certificates section of the corresponding hosted services.

- The certificates created by the sample application for SSL use are for demonstration purposes only and are not meant to be used in production.

- The management and SSL certificates .pfx files generated during installation should be kept in a safe location with strict permissions via access control lists (ACLs), or deleted after uploading them to Windows Azure.

**TO GENERATE THE WINDOWS AZURE MANAGEMENT
CERTIFICATE AND IMPORT IT FOR USE IN VISUAL STUDIO**

1. Go to the Windows Azure profile generation site at *http://go.microsoft.com/ fwlink/?LinkId=229563*.

2. Sign in to your Windows Live® account that has a Windows Azure subscription.

3. Start Visual Studio as an administrator. To do this, right-click on **Microsoft Visual Studio 2010** and select **Run as administrator**.

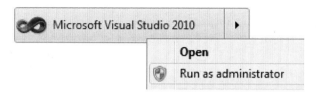

4. Open the Tailspin.sln solution.

5. Right-click on the Tailspin.Surveys.Cloud project and click **Publish**. Note that you will not complete the wizard yet; you will only perform some steps to generate and import the management certificate in preparation for the deployment.

6. In the Publish Windows Azure Application wizard page, click on the "**Sign in to download credentials**" link.

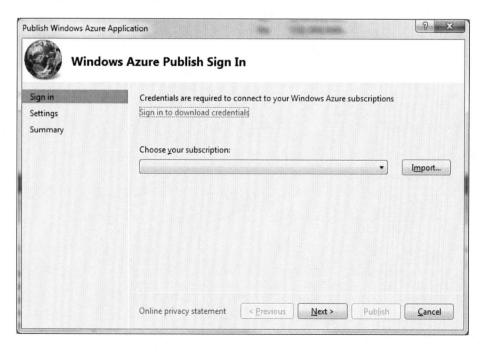

7. The link will open the Internet browser and navigate to the Windows Azure site. Sign in with a Windows Live account with a Windows Azure subscription.

8. Follow the steps on the page to download the .publishsettings file.

9. Return to the Publish Windows Azure Application wizard page in Visual Studio.

10. Click on the **Import** button and browse to the .publishsettings file you have just downloaded.

11. You can now click **Cancel** because you will need to prepare the solution before you can publish to Windows Azure.

    Note: *After this step, Visual Studio will be configured to publish to your Windows Azure subscription, and the management certificate will be installed in the Current User\My certificate store.*

TO EXPORT THE WINDOWS AZURE MANAGEMENT CERTIFICATE TO A .PFX FILE

1. Start the Microsoft Management Console (MMC).

2. Select **File**, select **Add/Remove Snap-in**.

3. In the Add or Remove Snap-ins dialog, from the Available snap-ins, select **Certificates**, and click **Add**.

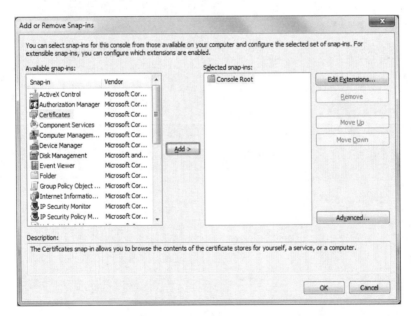

4. In the Certificates snap-in dialog, select **My user account**. Click **Finish**.

5. In the Add or Remove Snap-ins dialog, click **OK**.

6. In the MMC Console, select **Certificates - Current User**.

7. Expand **Personal**, and select **Certificates**.

8. In the Microsoft Management Console certificates list, locate and right-click the **Windows Azure Tools** certificate that you imported in the previous steps, select **All Tasks**, and click **Export**.

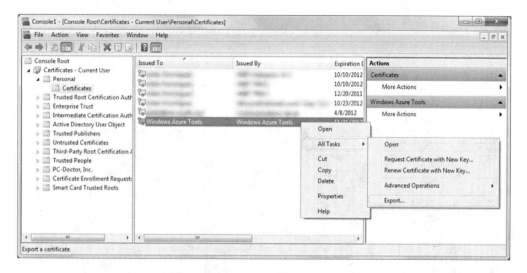

9. In the Certificate Export Wizard, click **Next**.

10. Click **Yes, export the private key**. Click **Next**.

11. Keep the **Personal Information Exchange –PKCS #12 (.PFX)** as the default. Click **Next**.

12. Enter a password for the exported file. Do not use a blank password because a password is mandatory when uploading a .pfx file to Windows Azure.

13. Enter the directory where the application is located and give it a name such as "C:\Tailspin\AzureManagementCert. pfx" and click **Next**.

14. Click **Finish**.

GENERATE THE SSL CERTIFICATE

1. Open a Visual Studio Command Prompt (2010) as an administrator (in the Windows 7 Start menu, type Visual Studio Command Prompt, select the "Visual Studio Command Prompt (2010)", right-click and select **Run as administrator**).

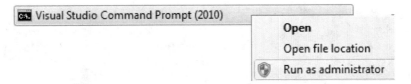

2. Change directories to the folder where you unzipped the source code for the Tailspin Surveys application.

3. To generate the SSL certificate, enter "GenerateSSLCert.cmd."

4. Enter a private key password for the certificate file. This is mandatory.

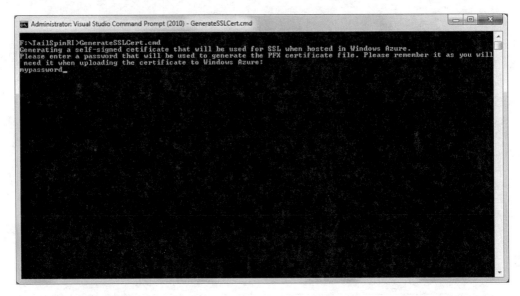

5. A window will pop up asking you to provide another password. Keep this blank and click **OK**.

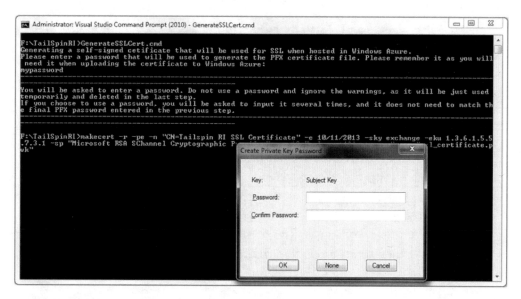

6. You will see a popup to confirm the creation of the certificate without password protection. Click **Yes**, because this latter password would only be used temporarily, but the generated .pfx file will use the password you entered in the previous step.

7. After completing these steps, you will have the SSL certificate in a file named ssl_certificate.pfx in your current directory.

CREATE THE REQUIRED HOSTED SERVICES
Next, you will need to create the hosted services.

TO CREATE THE REQUIRED HOSTED SERVICES

1. In the Management Portal - Windows Azure, click **Hosted Services, Storage Accounts & CDN** on the navigation bar on the left.

2. Click **Hosted Services** on the left menu.

3. Select your Windows Azure subscription.

4. Select **New Hosted Service**, either from the ribbon bar or on the context menu, by right-clicking on your Windows Azure subscription.

5. In the Create a New Hosted Service dialog:

   a. In the "Enter a name for your service" text box, enter **Tailspin-Surveys**.

   b. In the "Enter a URL prefix for your service" text box, enter a name of your choice to signify that this is the Tailspin web application. This prefix must be unique.

    c. Select **Create a new affinity group** from the "Create or choose an affinity group" drop-down menu.

    d. In the **Create a New Affinity Group** dialog, enter an Affinity group name and select a Location, and press **OK**.

    e. Select **Do not deploy.**

    f. Click **OK**.

6. Select the Windows Azure subscription to create the second hosted service.

7. In the **Create a New Hosted Service** dialog:

    a. In the "Enter a name for your service" text box, enter **Tailspin-Autoscaling**.

    b. In the "Enter a URL prefix for your service" text box, enter a name of your choice to signify that this is the Tailspin Autoscaling management website and run-time worker role. This prefix must be unique.

    c. Select the Affinity group that you created in the previous step from the "Create or choose an affinity group" drop-down menu.

    d. Select "**Do not deploy.**"

    e. Click **OK**.

You should see the two hosted services.

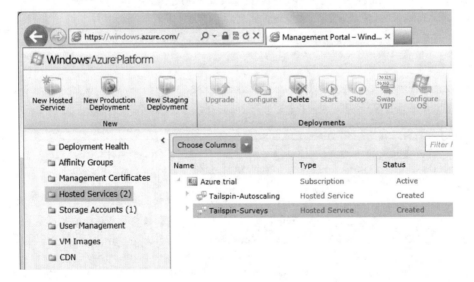

Upload Certificates as Hosted Services' Service Certificates

The cloud projects you will deploy to Windows Azure use the service certificates that must be uploaded to the Windows Azure service management certificates store. They are the secure sockets layer (SSL) certificates the websites use and the Windows Azure management certificate the Autoscaling Application Block uses to govern the number of instances of configured roles.

TO ADD THE CERTIFICATES

1. Add the SSL certificate to the Tailspin-Surveys hosted service.

   a. In the Management Portal - Windows Azure, select the Certificates folder under the **Tailspin-Surveys** hosted service and click **Add Certificate**.

   b. In the Upload an X.509 Certificate dialog, browse to the ssl_certificate.pfx certificate that was generated previously.

   c. Enter the password. Click **OK**.

   d. You should see the **Tailspin RI SSL Certificate** certificate added to the service certificates list on the portal.

2. Add the SSL certificate to the Tailspin-Autoscaling hosted service.

   a. In the Management Portal - Windows Azure, select the Certificates folder under the **Tailspin-Autoscaling** hosted service and click **Add Certificate**.

   b. In the **Upload an X.509 Certificate** dialog, browse to the ssl_certificate. pfx certificate that was generated previously.

   c. Enter the password. Click **OK**.

   d. You should see the **Tailspin RI SSL Certificate** added to the service certificates list on the portal.

3. Add the management certificate for the Tailspin-Autoscaling hosted service.

   a. In the Management Portal - Windows Azure, select the Certificates folder under the **Tailspin-Autoscaling** hosted service and click **Add Certificate**.

   b. In the **Upload an X.509 Certificate** dialog, browse to the Azure ManagementCert.pfx certificate that you exported previously.

   c. Enter the password. Click **OK**.

   d. You should see the **Windows Azure Tools** certificate added to the service certificates list on the portal.

You should see the hosted services with the certificates, as shown in the following image.

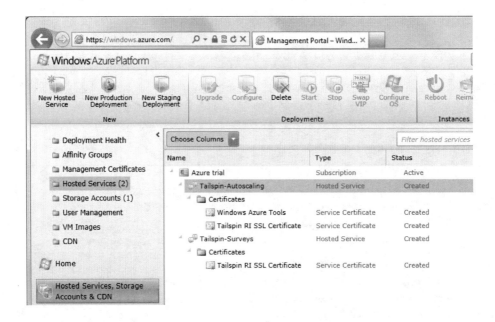

CREATE THE STORAGE ACCOUNT

The Autoscaling Application Block uses Windows Azure storage for its operations. For more information about autoscaling and how the Autoscaling Application Block works, see Chapter 4, *"Autoscaling and Windows Azure,"* in this guide. In this step you will create the storage account that the Autoscaling Application Block will use in the Tailspin scenario.

TO CREATE THE STORAGE ACCOUNT

1. In the Management Portal - Windows Azure, select **Storage Accounts**.
2. Select the correct subscription, right-click, and select **New Storage Account**.
3. In the Create a New Storage Account dialog,
   a. Choose a subscription.
   b. Enter a URL.
   c. Choose a region or affinity group you created previously.
   d. Click **OK**.

You should see the added storage account.

> **Note:** *You should make note of the name of the storage account because you will need it to configure your Visual Studio solution.*

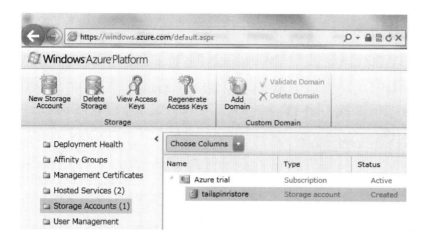

TO MAKE SURE THE APPLICATION USES THE CREATED STORAGE ACCOUNT

1. In Visual Studio, for each of the cloud projects' roles, double-click the role, and click on the **Configuration** tab.

2. Clear the check box "Use publish storage account as connection string when you publish to Windows Azure" if it is checked (it should not be checked).

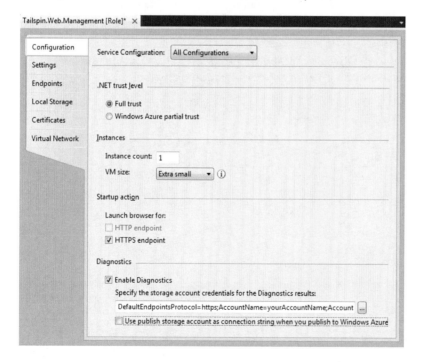

Building the Solution

Before you can build the solution, you need to:
1. Install NuGet packages.
2. Modify the certificates in the Visual Studio Cloud Projects.
3. Prepare the settings in the Cloud Projects.

INSTALL NUGET PACKAGES

The Tailspin Surveys application depends on certain binaries that are not included in the .zip file. Perform the following steps to download and install these dependencies using the **NuGet Package Manager**.

TO INSTALL NUGET PACKAGES
1. Start Visual Studio as an administrator. To do this, right-click on **Microsoft Visual Studio 2010** and select **Run as administrator**.

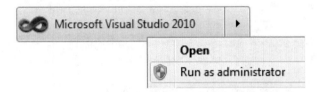

2. Open the Tailspin.sln solution.
3. In Solution Explorer, right-click the Tailspin solution, select **Enable NuGet Package Restore**, and click **Yes** in the confirmation dialog box.

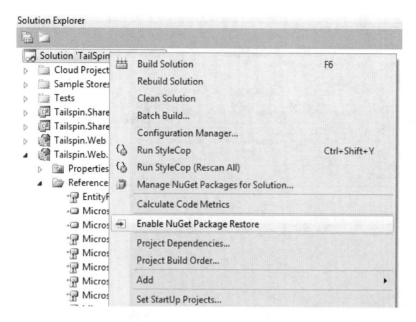

Note: *If you are using NuGet version 1.5 or earlier, you will not see the* **Enable NuGet Package Restore** *menu item. In this case, enter the following commands on the NuGet Package Manager Console. You can access the NuGet Package Manager Console through the Visual Studio menu. Point to* **Tools***, point to* **Library Package Manager***, select* **Package Manager Console***, and enter the following commands:*

- Install-Package NuGetPowerTools
- Enable-PackageRestore

MODIFY THE CERTIFICATES IN THE VISUAL STUDIO CLOUD PROJECTS

The Cloud projects in the Tailspin scenario use various certificates you have uploaded to Windows Azure in the previous sections. In this step, you will modify the Cloud projects to correctly refer to those certificates for the roles.

TO MODIFY THE CERTIFICATES IN THE VISUAL STUDIO CLOUD PROJECTS

1. In Visual Studio, in the Solution Explorer, select the **Tailspin.Web** role under the Tailspin.Surveys.Cloud project.

   a. Double-click the **Tailspin.Web** role and click **Certificates**.

   b. You should make the thumbprint for **ssl_certificate** match the thumbprint for **Tailspin RI SSL Certificate** in the Management Portal - Windows Azure. Update the thumbprint in Visual Studio, copying the value from the portal. Also make sure the Store Location is set to **LocalMachine**, and Store Name is set to **My**.

SSL certificate thumbprint in Visual Studio

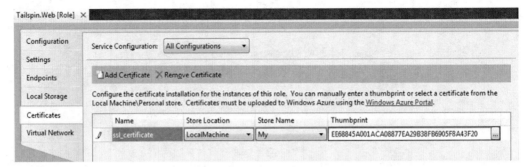

SSL certificate thumbprint in Windows Azure

2. Double-click the **Tailspin.Web.Management** role under the Tailspin.Autoscaling. Cloud project, select **Certificates**, and ensure that the thumbprint for the **ssl_certificate** corresponds to the thumbprint for the **Tailspin RI SSL Certificate** in the Management Portal - Windows Azure.

3. Double-click the **Tailspin.Workers.Autoscaling** role under the Tailspin.Auto-scaling.Cloud project, select **Certificates**, and ensure that the thumbprint for the **TailspinManagementCert** corresponds to the thumbprint for the **Windows Azure Tools** certificate in the Management Portal - Windows Azure.

PREPARE THE SETTINGS IN THE CLOUD PROJECTS

In this step, you will need to update the settings in the Cloud projects to specify the storage account you created previously.

TO PREPARE THE SETTINGS IN THE CLOUD PROJECTS

1. In the Management Portal - Windows Azure, select **Storage Accounts**.

2. Select the storage account that you created previously.

   a. On the right-hand side, under Primary access key, click **View**.

   b. In the View Storage Access Keys, copy the **Primary access key**.

3. In Visual Studio, double-click the **Tailspin.Web** role in the Tailspin.Surveys.Cloud project and click **Settings**.

   a. In the Service Configuration drop-down, select **All Configurations**.

   b. Ensure that the setting type for **DataConnectionString** is **Connection String**.

   c. Click the ellipsis (..) button to the right of the **DataConnectionString Value** field.

      i. In the Storage Account Connection String dialog, select **Enter storage account credentials**.

      ii. Update the **Account name** with the corresponding name of the storage account that you created previously.

      iii. Update the **Account key** with the primary access key copied in step 2.

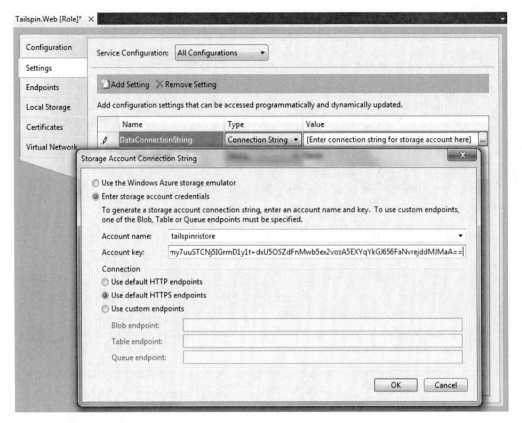

4. Update the connection string values to use the same value for all the following role settings:

   Note: *You will need to update the connection string value in several settings. Instead of using the Storage Account Connection String dialog every time, you can copy the value of the connection string you created in the previous step, and paste it into the* **Value** *field for the remaining settings.*

Role	Setting Name
Tailspin.Web	DataConnectionString
Tailspin.Web	Microsoft.WindowsAzure.Plugins. Diagnostics.ConnectionString
Tailspin.Web.Survey.Public	DataConnectionString
Tailspin.Web.Survey.Public	Microsoft.WindowsAzure.Plugins. Diagnostics.ConnectionString
Tailspin.Workers.Surveys	DataConnectionString
Tailspin.Workers.Surveys	Microsoft.WindowsAzure.Plugins. Diagnostics.ConnectionString
Tailspin.Web.Management	DataConnectionString
Tailspin.Web.Management	Microsoft.WindowsAzure.Plugins. Diagnostics.ConnectionString
Tailspin.Web.Management	AutoscalingStorage
Tailspin.Wokers.Autoscaling	DataConnectionString
Tailspin.Wokers.Autoscaling	Microsoft.WindowsAzure.Plugins. Diagnostics.ConnectionString
Tailspin.Wokers.Autoscaling	AutoscalingStorage

TO CREATE A PASSWORD FOR ACCESSING THE AUTOSCALING MANAGEMENT SITE

1. In Visual Studio, double-click the **Tailspin.Web.Management** role in the Tailspin. Autoscaling.Cloud project and click **Settings**.

2. Set a username and a password in the provided settings.

   Note: *Setting a password is mandatory for security reasons.*

BUILD THE SOLUTION
At this point, you are now ready to build the Tailspin solution.

TO BUILD THE SOLUTION

1. In the Visual Studio Solution Explorer, select the Tailspin solution in Visual Studio.

2. Right-click and select **Rebuild Solution**.

Deploy to Windows Azure

The following projects need to be deployed to Windows Azure:
- Tailspin.Surveys.Cloud (to the Tailspin-Surveys hosted service)
- Tailspin.Autoscaling.Cloud (to the Tailspin-Austoscaling hosted service)

Once you've deployed one project, you can deploy the next one as soon as you see that the deployment was added and has started in the Visual Studio Windows Azure Activity Log window.

> **Known Issue**: *Due to a* limitation in Visual Studio 2010 IntelliTrace, *the following runtime exception is thrown when the application block is hosted on Windows Azure with IntelliTrace enabled:*
> *System.Security.VerificationException: Operation could destabilize the runtime.*
> **Workaround**: *To address this issue, you will need to disable IntelliTrace on the Autoscaling Application Block assembly. To do this, add Microsoft.Practices.EnterpriseLibrary.WindowsAzure.* to the list of excluded modules. See instructions here: VerificationException from Windows Azure IntelliTrace.*

DEPLOYING TAILSPIN TO THE STAGING SLOT

You will first deploy these projects to the Staging deployment slot in your hosted service because the default values in the service information store for Tailspin Surveys reference the deployment in the Staging slot.

TO DEPLOY TAILSPIN TO THE STAGING SLOT
1. In Solution Explorer, right-click the **TailSpin.Surveys.Cloud** project and select **Publish**.

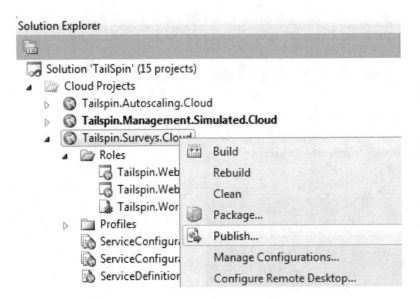

2. In the Publish Windows Azure Application wizard, select the following:

   a. In the Windows Azure Publish Sign In step, select the subscription you imported in the previous steps, and click **Next**.

   b. In the Windows Azure Publish Settings step, select **Tailspin-Surveys** as the Hosted service.

   c. Select **Staging** as the Environment.

   d. In the Service configuration, select **Cloud**.

   e. Click **Publish** to publish the hosted service.

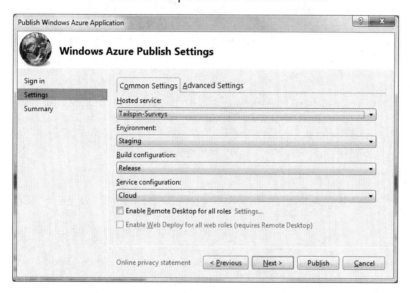

3. Before continuing with the next step, wait until the project finishes building and you see that the deployment was added and has started in the Visual Studio Windows Azure Activity Log window.

4. In Solution Explorer, right-click the **Tailspin.Autoscaling.Cloud** project and select **Publish**.

5. In the Publish Windows Azure Application wizard, select the following:

   a. In the Windows Azure Publish Sign In step, select the subscription you imported in the previous steps, and click **Next**.

   b. In the Windows Azure Publish Settings step, select **Tailspin-Autoscaling** as the Hosted service.

   c. Select **Staging** as the Environment.

   d. In the Service configuration, select **Cloud**.

   e. Click **Publish** to publish the hosted service.

Testing If Tailspin Surveys Works

You should ensure that the Tailspin Surveys application works from a public website, tenant website, and management website.

Public Website

Tailspin contains a public website that allows end users to fill out surveys. To view this site, browse to the hosted service for Tailspin-Surveys.

http://[dns for Tailspin-Surveys hosted service]

You can find this URL in the Management Portal - Windows Azure. Go into the Hosted Services section and select the Tailspin.Surveys.Cloud deployment that is under the Tailspin-Surveys hosted service. You will see the DNS name on the details on the right, and you can right-click and copy this value.

Tenant Website

Tenants can access the tenant website. This website allows the tenants to create surveys and analyze the results. There are two tenants provisioned: Adatum and Fabrikam.

To view this site, browse to the hosted service for Tailspin-Surveys using HTTPS. You can find this URL in the Management Portal - Windows Azure.

https://[dns for Tailspin-Surveys hosted service]

The URL is the same as the public website, but you need to change the scheme from HTTP to HTTPS.

Because the solution uses a test certificate, you will see the message: "Continue to this website (not recommended)." Click on this link to continue.

When you browse to this site, you will be logged on using (simulated) claims-based authentication.

Management Website

Tailspin operators can use the management website to manage rules and monitor the autoscaling process. There is also a page to generate a simulated load on the website, to show how the autoscaling process works.

To view this site, browse to the hosted service for Tailspin-Autoscaling using HTTPS.

https://[dns for Tailspin-Autoscaling hosted service]

You can find this URL in the Management Portal - Windows Azure. Go into the Hosted Services section and select the Tailspin.Autoscaling.Cloud deployment that is under the Tailspin-Autoscaling hosted service. You will see the DNS name on the details on the right, and you can right-click and copy this value, but make sure to update the scheme to use HTTPS instead of HTTP.

Because the solution uses a test certificate, you will see the message: "Continue to this website (not recommended)." Click on this link to continue.

Configuring Tailspin Autoscaling Functionality

Now you are ready to configure the Service Information Store and upload the sample rules.

CONFIGURING THE SERVICE INFORMATION STORE

The Service Information Store specifies the roles in the application that can be scaled, as well as additional settings for the operation of the Autoscaling Application Block. In order to see the scenario running, you will need to configure the Service Information Store to match your newly created environment.

TO CONFIGURE THE SERVICE INFORMATION STORE

1. Navigate to the Tailspin management site.

2. Click the **Reset service model to default** link under the **Service Information XML file** heading in the Rules and Service Information Stores section. This option is only available on the Home page, not on the **Service Information** tab on the Navigation tab.

   Note: *This will upload to Blob storage a copy of the* **default-service-information-set.xml** *file that is in the SourceCode\Tailspin\Sample stores folder in your installation location.*

3. The default service information file does not contain the correct subscription information, so click the **Service Information** tab on the navigation bar in order to update it to reflect your current deployment in Windows Azure.

4. Click the line on the **Subscriptions** list with the **TailspinSubscription** name. You will paste in the value from the next step here.

5. In the Management Portal - Windows Azure, select your subscription.

   a. On the right-hand pane, select and copy your subscription ID using Ctrl+C (the portal is a Microsoft Silverlight® browser plug-in application, so the right-click copy menu option is not available).

6. Paste the value into the **SubscriptionId** field on the **Subscription Details** form in the Tailspin management site.

7. In the Management Certificates section on the Management Portal - Windows Azure:

   a. Select the uploaded Tailspin management certificate with the name Windows Azure Tools.

   b. Select and copy the thumbprint of the certificate from the pane on the right-hand side.

   c. Paste the thumbprint value into the **Management Certificate Thumbprint** field on the **Subscription Details** form in the Tailspin management site.

8. In the Management Portal - Windows Azure, select **Tailspin-Surveys** Hosted Service.

a. Select the DNS Prefix value of the Hosted Service on the right-hand pane and copy the value.

b. Paste the value into the **DNS Prefix** field under the Deployed Hosted Services section in the Tailspin management site form.

9. In Visual Studio, double-click on the **Tailspin.Workers.Autoscaling** role under the Tailspin.Management.Worker.Cloud project roles.

a. Select the **Settings** tab.

b. Copy the value of the **AutoscalingStorage** setting.

c. Paste the value into the **Connection String** field under the **Storage Account** section in the Tailspin management site form.

10. Click the **Save** button at the bottom of the page.

UPLOADING THE SAMPLE RULES

1. On the Tailspin management site, click on the **Home** tab.

2. Click the **Reset rules to default** link under the **Rule Set XML file** heading in the Rules and Service Information stores section. This option is only available on the Home page, not on the **Service Information** tab on the Navigation tab.

   Note: *This will upload to Blob Storage a copy of the* **default-rules-set.xml** *file that is in the SourceCode\Tailspin\Sample stores folder in your installation location.*

After these steps, the Tailspin Surveys application should be automatically scaled based on the rules. You can go to the **Monitoring** tab to see how the target application evolves with time, or go into the corresponding tabs and change the reactive and constraint rules at run time to see how it behaves with different settings.

Running Tailspin Surveys Locally in Debug Mode

The Autoscaling Application Block uses the Windows Azure Storage functionality added during the SDK 1.6 timeframe, which is currently not supported by the Storage Emulator. Therefore, the local debug runs still need to access the live Windows Azure Storage account. This is why you needed to set all of the connection strings in the Prepare the Settings in the Cloud Projects section to target **All Configurations.**

Also, the Windows Azure Service Management API is not supported on the Compute Emulator, thus the Autoscaling Application Block can only target hosted services deployed to Windows Azure.

The **Tailspin.Autoscaling.Cloud** project can be run in debug mode locally, but it needs to use Windows Azure Storage for storing the data points and the target application must be hosted in Windows Azure.

Running the Management Application in Simulated Mode

If you wish, you can run the management application in simulated mode. This allows you to explore the management application without having to deploy the full Tailspin Surveys application to Windows Azure. This experimental mode is provided to present you with the option to concentrate on the Autoscaling Application Block's interactions, without including any Windows Azure-related extra steps.

The implementation replaces some classes through implementing the interfaces that the block accesses, as shown in the following figure:

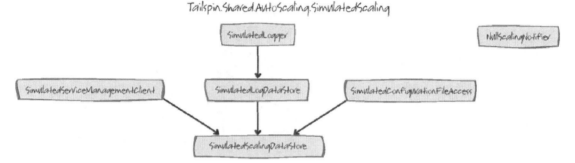

The solution uses an in-session storage, which is not durable across different sessions or debugs runs.

TO WORK IN THE SIMULATED MODE

1. Start Visual Studio as an administrator.

2. Open the Tailspin.Simulated.sln solution.

3. In Solution Explorer, right-click the Tailspin.Simulated solution, select **Enable NuGet Package Restore**, and click **Yes** in the confirmation dialog box.

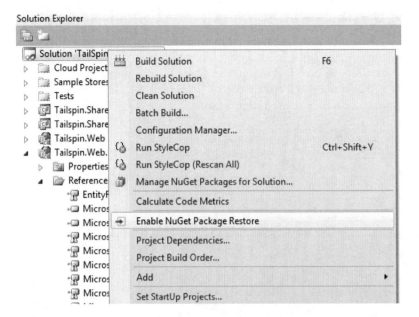

Note: *If you are using NuGet version 1.5 or less, you will not see the* **Enable NuGet Package Restore** *menu item. In this case, enter the following commands on the NuGet Package Manager Console. You can access the NuGet Package Manager Console through the Visual Studio menu. Point to* **Tools***, point to* **Library Package Manager***, select* **Package Manager Console***, and enter the following commands:*

- Install-Package NuGetPowerTools
- Enable-PackageRestore

4. Set the **Tailspin.Management.Simulated.Cloud** project as the startup project.

5. Press F5.

6. Because the solution uses a test certificate, you will see the following message in the browser window: "Continue to this website (not recommended)." Click on that link to continue.

7. You should see the "Simulated Scaling Mode is currently active" message on the lower left corner of the browser window.

Known Issues

The Tailspin Surveys application has the following known issues:
- If the rules and service information store XML files do not conform to the included schemas, the application throws an exception and stops working.
- Due to a *limitation in Visual Studio 2010 IntelliTrace*, the following runtime exception is thrown when the application block is hosted on Windows Azure with IntelliTrace enabled:

```
System.Security.VerificationException:
Operation could destabilize the runtime.
```

Workaround: *To address this issue, you will need to disable IntelliTrace on the Autoscaling Application Block assembly.*
To do this, add Microsoft.Practices.EnterpriseLibrary.Windows Azure.* to the list of excluded modules. See instructions here: VerificationException from Windows Azure IntelliTrace.

- Input field validation is currently incomplete.

More Information

Visit the Enterprise Library Integration Pack for Windows Azure home page for the latest news:
http://entlib.codeplex.com/wikipage?title=EntLib5Azure

Please refer to the installation documents of the previous releases for the topics that are not covered in this document:
http://wag.codeplex.com/releases/view/71446

To learn more about the Autoscaling Application Block, see Chapter 4, "Autoscaling and Windows Azure," in this guide and "The Autoscaling Application Block" on MSDN:
http://msdn.microsoft.com/en-us/library/hh680945(v=PandP.50).aspx

To view a video walkthrough about the Autoscaling Application Block, see "Autoscaling Windows Azure applications" on Channel 9:
http://channel9.msdn.com/posts/Autoscaling-Windows-Azure-applications

To learn more about the Transient Fault Handing Application Block, see Chapter 6, "Transient Fault Handling" in this guide and "The Transient Fault Handing Application Block" on MSDN:
http://msdn.microsoft.com/en-us/library/hh680934(v=PandP.50).aspx

To get the NuGet Package Manager, see the NuGet community site on CodePlex:
http://nuget.codeplex.com/

To learn more about Windows Azure profile generation, see
Windows Azure:
http://go.microsoft.com/fwlink/?LinkId=229563.

To learn more about the limitation in Visual Studio 2010 IntelliTrace and how to disable IntelliTrace on an assembly, see "RIA, Azure, and IntelliTrace" on Kyle McClellan's blog:
http://blogs.msdn.com/b/kylemc/archive/2010/06/09/ria-azure-and-intellitrace.aspx

To access web resources more easily, see the online version of the bibliography on MSDN:
http://msdn.microsoft.com/en-us/library/hh749032(v=PandP.50).aspx

APPENDIX C   Glossary

application throttling. The process of reducing an application's resource requirements, typically to maintain the performance of core functionality in response to changes in workload. Examples would be switching off nonessential features, or switching to a lightweight UI.

autoscaling. Using an automated mechanism to scale a Windows Azure™ technology platform application.

blob lease. A mechanism in Windows Azure that ensures that only a single client can access a blob.

burst. A sudden increase in the workload for a Windows Azure application.

cool-down period (in the context of the Autoscaling Application Block). The period of time after a scaling action has taken place against your Windows Azure application during which no further autoscaling activities should take place. This allows the application to settle down after the scaling operation and helps to reduce the number of scaling actions that are performed. You can configure the value of the cool-down period independently for scale-up and scale-down operations. The default value of the cool-down period is 20 minutes.

constraint rules. Rules that set explicit boundaries on the scaling process by defining the minimum and maximum number of instances permitted during a given time period. You should set the minimum value to ensure that you continue to meet your service level agreements (SLAs). You should set the maximum value in order to limit your costs. Constraint rules consist of the maximum and minimum instance count boundaries, a rank, and optionally a timetable that defines when the rule is in effect. If there is no timetable, the rule is always in effect.

cost optimization (in the context of the Autoscaling Application Block). A way to ensure that you make the best use of your running role instances by starting them early in the clock hour and stopping them late in the clock hour.

data point. An instantaneous metric value with an associated timestamp. The following table shows some example data points.

Metric	Value	Timestamp
CPU usage	83.7%	10:03:56
Unprocessed orders	2873	10:04:13

detection strategy (in the context of the Transient Fault Handling Application Block). A definition of the logic used to identify transient errors in a service.

elasticity. The ability of an application to automatically scale to meet changing workload requirements.

freeze period (in the context of the Autoscaling Application Block). The period immediately after a deployment operation or a change to your Windows Azure application's service configuration during which Windows Azure does not allow any additional configuration changes. The duration of the freeze period is determined by Windows Azure and is not configurable. The duration of the freeze period is typically a couple of minutes, but may vary.

horizontal scalability (in the context of the Autoscaling Application Block). The ability of your application to be scaled by adding more role instances to your hosted service.

management API certificate (in the context of Windows Azure). A certificate used to secure Windows Azure Management Service API calls.

metric. A parameter that is measured. Examples include performance counters such as CPU usage and free memory, and business-related metrics such as the number of unprocessed orders and the number of registered tenants in the application. Metrics may also be defined as the result of a calculation such as queue length per instance in the case where multiple role instances share a queue.

operand. Defines how to calculate the value for a metric that can be used in a reactive rule expression. For example, you can create a performance counter operand that monitors the CPU usage for a worker role and calculates the average value over 10 minutes. Operands are used by reactive rules.

rank. A property of a rule that is used by the block to resolve conflicts between rules. The higher the rank, the higher the priority.

reactive rules. Rules that react to varying loads on your application and trigger a scaling action when an aggregate value derived from a set of data points exceeds a certain threshold.

retry strategy (in the context of the Transient Fault Handling Application Block). A definition of how many retries to attempt and the interval between each retry.

retry policy (in the context of the Transient Fault Handling Application Block). The combination of a retry strategy and a detection strategy.

role. A service definition to deploy your application code to Windows Azure. A Windows Azure application may consist of many web and worker roles.

role instance. An instance of a web or worker role running in Windows Azure. An individual web or worker role may have multiple running instances in order to make the role more reliable or capable of handling larger workloads.

scale group. A way to define autoscaling rules that can act on multiple roles at once. Scale groups help to minimize the number of rules you need to create and manage. They can include roles in different hosted services.

service certificate (in the context of Windows Azure). A certificate that an application running in Windows Azure can use to encrypt or decrypt data.

service information. Defines the aspects of your Windows Azure application that are relevant to the Autoscaling Application Block. For example, the Autoscaling Application Block uses the service information file to know which roles are available for scaling, or which queues are available for monitoring.

stabilization (in the context of the Autoscaling Application Block). Damping the scaling operations to prevent unnecessary oscillations in the number of role instances as a consequence of the autoscaling operations.

target (in the context of the Autoscaling Application Block). Identifies a web or worker role type that can have multiple running instances and that can be scaled. Autoscaling actions can specify changes to the instance count of a target when the action is performed by an autoscaling rule. Targets usually refer to roles in a different hosted service from the hosted service where the Autoscaling Application Block is hosted.

timetable (in the context of the Autoscaling Application Block). Determines when a constraint rule is active. If a constraint rule does not have a timetable, the rule will always be on.

transient fault. An error that is due to some transient condition. For example, a transient fault can occur when you use a cloud-hosted service such as Windows Azure storage or SQL Azure™ technology platform and you lose your connection as a result of temporary resource shortages. The result is an error condition, but when you retry the same command a short time later, it may succeed because the connection has been restored.

vertical scalability (in the context of the Autoscaling Application Block). The ability for your application to be scaled by increasing the size of a role instance by using more CPU cores and/or more memory.

WASABiCmdlets. A collection of Windows PowerShell® Cmdlets that you can use to manage the Autoscaling Application Block.

Index

A

.cscfg file, 93

.pfx file, 162-165

Access Control (ACS), 6

actions *see* custom actions

ActiveSurveysDataPointsCollector class, 121-124

activeSurveysOperand custom operand, 119-121

advanced usage scenarios, 60-66

Appendix A *see* Tailspin Surveys to multiple data centers

Appendix B *see* Tailspin Surveys installation guide

applications

    developing, 7-8

    differences, 131-132

    lifecycle, 63-64

    Tailspin Surveys, 23-25

    throttling, 35-36

    updating, 9

architecture, 27-28

audience, xvi

autoscaling, 31-81

    adding to VS project, 49

    application throttling, 35-36

    collecting history data, 91

    configuration UI, 92

    constraint rules, 36-39

    constraint rules interacting with reactive rules, 41

    constraint rules with maximum and minimum values, 39

    instances, 34-35, 54-55

    lifecycle, 43-45

    logging, 42-43

    monitoring, 59

    multiple constraint rules and no reactive rules, 38

    NuGet, 49

    predictability, 46

    reactive rules, 39-42

    rules, 55-57

    solution, 86-92

    Surveys elasticity, 95

    visualizing actions, 111-114

    when to use and not use, 45-47

Autoscaling Application Block, xv, 20

    adding throttling behavior, 54

    advanced usage scenarios, 60-66

    application lifecycle, 63-64

    autoscaling rules, 55-57

    average rule evaluation period, 69-70

    changing Windows Azure application, 51

    configuration settings, 67-71

    custom actions, 65

    custom logging, 66

    custom operands, 65

    custom stores, 66

    Data Collector, 74-75

    Data Collector activity, 75

    Data Points Store, 75

    different ratios at different times, 61-62

    extending, 65-66

    hosting, 50-51

    how it works, 73-76

    instance autoscaling throttling, 54-55

    instance scaling, 33

    Logger component, 76

    long rule evaluation period, 70

    Metronome, 74

monitoring, 58-60
notifications, 62-63
planning tool, 72-73
Rule Evaluator activity, 75
Rules Store, 75-76
scale groups, 60-61, 88
Scaler, 76
schedule-based autoscaling without reactive
    rules, 57-58
service information, 52-53
Service Information Store, 75
stabilizer configuring, 70-71
Tailspin scenario, 86-92
throttling, 33
timing relationships, 68
Tracker activity, 76
using, 47-71
WASABiCmdlets, 66
average rule evaluation period, 69-70
AzureStorageWadLogDataStore class, 114

B
Beth *see* business manager role
Bharath *see* cloud specialist role
bibliography, 16
billing configuration for a standard subscription, 11
Binary Large Object (BLOB) Service, 4
bursts, 83-85
Business Intelligence Reporting service, 7
business manager role, xix

C
Caching Application Block, 18
Caching Service, 5
certificates
    and deployment, 126
    to enable scaling operations, 127
    as hosted services' service certificates,
        169-170
    service certificate to enable SSL, 126-127
    in the Visual Studio Cloud projects, 173-175
    see also SSL certificates
cloud, 1
Cloud projects setting, 175-177
cloud specialist role, xviii
CloudStorageAccount class, 93
community support, xxii, 12-16
compute environment, 3-4

conditional retry logic, 134
configuration
    differences, 131
    settings, 67-71
    stabilizer, 70-71
constraint rules, 32-33
    autoscaling, 36-39
    interacting with reactive rules, 41
    with maximum and minimum values, 39
    multiple with no reactive rules, 38
    Surveys elasticity, 88-91, 95-96
Content Delivery Network (CDN), 5
contributors and reviewers, xxi-xxii
cool-down periods, 52-53
costs
    estimating, 12
    managing, 46
Cryptography Application Block, 18
.cscfg file, 93
custom actions
    Autoscaling Application Block, 65
    Surveys elasticity, 115-119
    Tailspin Surveys rule editor, 118-119
customer demand, 45
custom logging, 66
custom operands
    Autoscaling Application Block, 65
    Surveys elasticity, 119-124
    with the Tailspin Surveys rule editor, 124
custom services, 140
custom stores, 66

D
Data Access Application Block, 18
data center costs, 130-131
Data Collector, 74-75
Data Collector activity, 75
data management, 4-5
Data Points Store, 75
debug mode, 182
definitions, 187-190
Dependency Checking tool, 126, 160-161
different ratios at different times, 61-62

E
Ed *see* Enterprise Library expert role
Enterprise Library
    components, 19

described, 17-21
Enterprise Library expert role, xix
Enterprise Library Integration Pack, 17-21
Exception Handling Application Block, 18
extending, 65-66
extensionAssemblies element, 124

F
faults *see* transient faults
feedback and support, 13
foreword, xi-xii
FromConfigurationSetting method, 93
functionality, 181

G
glossary, 187-190
goals and concerns, 26-27
GraphController class, 112-114
guide, xv

H
HomeController class, 110
horizontal scalability, 2
hosted services, 167
hosting
    Autoscaling Application Block, 50-51
    code creating services, 167-168
how to use this guide, xv

I
inside the implementation, 92-125
instance autoscaling rules, 54-55
instances, 34-35
    instantiating objects, 137
    scaling, 33
IntelliTrace, 178, 184-185
introduction, 1-16
IT professional role, xix

J
Jana *see* software architect role

K
known issues, 184-185

L
lifecycle, 43-45

Logger component, Autoscaling Application Block, 76
logging
    autoscaling, 42-43
    configuration, 124-125
    see also custom logging
Logging Application Block, 18
logic, 134
long rule evaluation period, 70

M
management website, 180
Marketplace service, 7
Markus *see* software developer role
Metronome, 74
Microsoft Enterprise Library Integration Pack
    for Windows Azure *see* Enterprise Library
    Integration Pack
monitoring, 58-60
multiple geographic locations, 128-132

N
networking services, 5-6
notifications, 62-63
    by SMS, 92
NuGet, 49, 184
    packages, 172-173

O
objects, 137
online bibliography, 16
operands, 40, 101
    see also custom operands
option 1: deploying centrally, 129
option 2: deploying in each data center, 130

P
password for autoscaling management site, 177
performance counter data, 102-104
.pfx file, 162-165
planning tool, 72-73
Poe *see* IT professional role
Policy Injection Application Block, 18
predictability, 46
preface, xv-xix
prerequisites, xvii-xviii
    Tailspin Surveys installation guide, 160
public website, 180

Q

Queue Service, 4

R

reactive rules, 32-33
    autoscaling, 39-42
reactive scaling rules, 96-99
reactive throttling rules, 99-100
reading and writing to the rules store, 107-109
REST-based interfaces, 8
retries
    default retry strategies, 146
    defining retry strategies, 137-138
    policy, 138-139
    strategies, 134, 146
retry logic, 134
RetryManager class, 138
    Surveys resilience, 146
RetryPolicy class, 139
reviewers, xxi-xxii
roles, xviii-xix
    instances, 131
    Tailspin role types, 88
Rule Evaluator activity, 75
RuleModelStore class, 146-147
rules
    average rule evaluation period, 69-70
    constraint vs. reactive, 37
    editing and saving rules, 107-110
    instance autoscaling rules, 54-55
    locating the rules store, 107
    long rule evaluation period, 70
    reading and writing to the rules store, 107-109
    sample rules upload, 182
    valid rules, 109
    see also constraint rules; reactive rules
RuleSetModelStore class, 146
RuleSetSerializer class, 107-109
Rules Store, 75-76

S

samples
    configuration settings, 67-71
    rule uploading, 182
scale groups, 60-62, 88
Scaler, 76
scaling out, 31

scaling up, 31
scenarios
    advanced usage scenarios, 60-66
    see also Tailspin scenario
schedule-based autoscaling without reactive rules, 57-58
Security Application Block, 18
Service Bus, Windows Azure, 6
service certificate to enable SSL, 126-127
service information, 52-53
    definition, 93-95
    editing and saving, 111
ServiceInformationModelStore class, 111
Service Information Store, 75
Service Information Store configuring, 181-182
services
    Caching Service, 5
    code creating services, 167-168
    custom services, 140
    and features, 3-7
    hosted services, 167
    networking services, 5-6
    Queue Service, 4
    see also custom services
setup and deployment, 126-132
SharedContainerBootstrapper class, 107
single data center, 129
software architect role, xviii
Software as a Service (SaaS), 25
software developer role, xix
source code and dependencies, 160-161
SQL Azure, 2
    managing database, 9
SQL Azure Database, 5
SQL Azure Data Sync, 5
SSL certificates, 165-167
    thumbprints, 174
stabilizer configuring, 70-71
Staging deployment slot, 178-179
storage account creation, 170-171
stores *see* custom stores
subscriptions
    and billing model, 10-11
    Windows Azure subscription deployment, 162-171
support, 12-16
Surveys elasticity, 83-132
    ActiveSurveysDataPointsCollector class, 121-124

activeSurveysOperand custom operand, 119-121

application differences, 131-132

autoscaling, 95

autoscaling configuration UI, 92

autoscaling solution, 86-92

certificates and deployment, 126

collecting autoscaling history data, 91

configuration differences, 131

constraint rules, 88-91, 95-96

creating valid rules, 109

.cscfg file, 93

custom actions, 115-119

custom actions and Tailspin Surveys rule editor, 118-119

custom operands, 119-124

custom operand with the Tailspin Surveys rule editor, 124

data center costs, 130-131

Dependency Checking tool, 126

editing and saving rules, 107-110

extensionAssemblies element, 124

GraphController class, 112-114

inside the implementation, 92-125

locating the rules store, 107

logging configuration, 124-125

management certificate to enable scaling operations, 127

multiple geographic locations, 128-132

notifications by SMS, 92

operands, 101

option 1: deploying centrally, 129

option 2: deploying in each data center, 130

overview, 86-92

performance counter data, 102-104

reactive scaling rules, 96-99

reactive throttling rules, 99-100

reading and writing to the rules store, 107-109

role instances, 131

service certificate to enable SSL, 126-127

service information definition, 93-95

service information editing and saving, 111

setup and deployment, 126-132

single data center, 129

throttling behavior, 105-106

TransferSurveysToSqlAzureCommand class, 106

validating target names in the rule definitions, 110

visualizing the autoscaling actions, 111-114

WebRole class, 102-104

see also Tailspin Surveys installation guide; Tailspin Surveys to multiple data centers

SurveySqlStore class, 147

Surveys resilience, 143-148

default retry strategies, 146

RetryManager class, 146

retry strategies, 146

RuleSetModelStore class, 146

SurveySqlStore class, 147

Transient Fault Handling Application Block, 144-148

see also Tailspin Surveys installation guide; Tailspin Surveys to multiple data centers

T

Tailspin scenario, 23-29

architecture, 27-28

Autoscaling Application Block, 86-92

goals and concerns, 26-27

role types, 88

Tailspin Surveys installation guide, 159-185

certificates as hosted services' service certificates, 169-170

certificates in the Visual Studio Cloud projects, 173-175

configuring functionality, 181

debug mode, 182

hosted services creation, 167-168

known issues, 184-185

management application in simulated mode, 183-184

management certificates and exporting as .pfx file, 162-165

management website, 180

NuGet packages, 172-173

password for autoscaling management site, 177

prerequisites, 160

public website, 180

sample rules uploading, 182

Service Information Store configuring, 181-182

settings in the Cloud projects, 175-177

source code and dependencies, 160-161

SSL certificate, 165-167

SSL certificate thumbprint in Visual Studio, 174
SSL certificate thumbprint in Windows Azure, 174
Staging deployment slot, 178-179
storage account creation, 170-171
tenant website, 180
testing, 180
Windows Azure deployment, 178-180
Windows Azure subscription deployment, 162-171
see also Surveys elasticity; Surveys resilience
Tailspin Surveys to multiple data centers, 149-157
    Option 1, 149-154
    Option 2, 154-157
Tailspin.Web.Management project, 110
Tailspin.Web role, 126-127
team, xxi-xxii
tenant website, 180
terminology, 187-190
testing, 180
throttling, 33
    applications, 35-36
    instance autoscaling throttling, 54-55
    reactive throttling rules, 99-100
throttling behavior
    Autoscaling Application Block, 54
    Surveys elasticity, 105-106
ThrottlingMode, 105
thumbprints, 174
timing relationships, 68
Topaz *see* Transient Fault Handling Application Block
Tracker activity, 76
TransferSurveysToSqlAzureCommand class, 106
Transient Fault Handling Application Block, xv, 20
    custom services, 140
    defining retry strategies, 137-138
    diagram, 135
    history, 135
    instantiating objects, 137
    retry policy, 138-139
    Surveys resilience, 144-148
    transient faults, 134-136
    using, 136-139
    Visual Studio project, 136
    when to use, 140
transient faults, 133-142

conditional retry logic, 134
historical note, 135
Transient Fault Handling Application Block, 134-136
see also Transient Fault Handling Application Block

U

Unity Dependency Injection and Interception, 18

V

validating target names in the rule definitions, 110
Validation Application Block, 18
vertical scalability, 2
Virtual Machine (VM role), 3-4
Virtual Network Connect, 5-6
Virtual Network Traffic Manager, 6
Visual Studio project, 136
vocabulary, 187-190
VS project, 49

W

WADPerformanceCountersTable, 102
WASABi *see* Autoscaling Application Block
WASABiCmdlets, 66
WebRole class, 102-104
websites, 180
when to use and not use, 45-47
who's who, xvi
Windows Azure, 1-2
    Access Control (ACS), 6
    billing configuration for a standard subscription, 11
    Binary Large Object (BLOB) Service, 4
    Business Intelligence Reporting service, 7
    Caching Service, 5
    changing application, 51
    compute environment, 3-4
    Content Delivery Network (CDN), 5
    cost estimating, 12
    data management, 4-5
    developing applications, 7-8
    Marketplace service, 7
    networking services, 5-6
    other services, 7
    Queue Service, 4
    Service Bus, 6
    services and features, 3-7

SQL Azure Database, 5
SQL Azure Data Sync, 5
subscription and billing model, 10-11
updating applications, 9
Virtual Machine (VM role), 3-4
Virtual Network Connect, 5-6
Virtual Network Traffic Manager, 6
Windows Azure Compute (Web and Worker
    Roles), 3
Windows Azure Drives, 4
Windows Azure Storage, 4-5
Windows Azure Table Service, 4
Windows Azure Compute (Web and Worker
    Roles), 3
Windows Azure deployment, 178-180
Windows Azure Drives, 4
Windows Azure Storage, 4-5
Windows Azure subscription deployment, 162-171
Windows Azure Table Service, 4